A Revolut
Road Map

This is a book for women of today who face completely new and different decisions. *Good Guys, Bad Guys and Other Lovers* is witty, explicit and helpful! For example:

- Are you in a difficult relationship? What's wrong? Pinpointing previously misunderstood patterns, here is a totally new way of looking at what is *really* going on – plus a new vocabulary to talk about it all with your lover.
- Are you happy being single, but worried that AIDS is only one lover away? With this book you can avoid the pitfalls of being single and shrug off the new conservative pressures to 'settle down'.
- Do you want to transform a one-night stand into a meaningful relationship? This book will show you how to do that too!

If you've been told once too often that you 'love too much' – and you are ready to throw any new advice book out of the window – this one is for you. Irreverent, radically new and – unlike the others – it doesn't tell women they are to blame and that *they* should change.

- Packed with practical tips on how to deal with the most sticky situations – in bed and out
- Helps with those agonizing decisions about whether to stay in your relationship

Check out the personal questions on pp. 63–4, 90–1, 105–6, 128–9 and 188–9 to help you think through your own situation. And write to us! (See page 193.)

GOOD GUYS
BAD GUYS
AND OTHER
LOVERS

EVERY WOMAN'S GUIDE TO RELATIONSHIPS

SHERE HITE
KATE COLLERAN

PANDORA

LONDON SYDNEY WELLINGTON

First published by Pandora Press, an imprint of the Trade Division of Unwin Hyman, in 1989.

PANDORA PRESS
Unwin Hyman Ltd
15/17 Broadwick Street, London W1V 1FP

Allen & Unwin Australia Pty Ltd
P.O. Box 764, 8 Napier Street, North Sydney, NSW 2060, Australia

Allen & Unwin NZ Ltd (in association with the Port Nicholson Press)
Compusales Building, 75 Ghuznee Street, Wellington, New Zealand

British Library Cataloguing in Publication Data

Hite, Shere and Colleran, Kate Lee
I. Title
Good guys, bad guys and other lovers:
every woman's guide to relationships
306.7

ISBN 0-04-440364-X

Set in 10 on 11 point Palatino by Computape (Pickering) Ltd and printed by Cox and Wyman Ltd., Reading.

Contents

CONTENTS

CONTENTS

—1—

Loving Men in the 1990s: Changing the Emotional Contract

RENAMING WHAT GOES ON IN RELATIONSHIPS

There are certain patterns of feelings and events that emerge repeatedly as women describe their relationships with men. The feelings are those we all recognize, but the patterns have not been accurately depicted – at least, not as women define them.

Here are some of the most confusing situations women describe in relationships – and a new interpretation of what they mean. How often have you heard women say things like this:

> I try to open him up. I want to talk about our relationship, feelings and problems, develop solutions or compromises. He is quiet, so I have to initiate it and drag it out of him. I usually work the hardest to resolve the problem. Sometimes, when he finds it hard to express himself, he withdraws. Without communicating, how can you solve anything?

> I love him and I know he loves me. I always tell him that he should tell me anything he wants to. He never tells me when he's down or depressed. He says he doesn't want to bother anyone with his problems. But I would love for both of us to share everything with each other.

1

One young woman remembers an early relationship in which she felt anxious and uncertain, but was never quite sure why:

When I was 15 I met Charlie. It was an instant crush. Our first 'date' was arranged through his friends talking to my friends. The date consisted of him coming over to my house one summer afternoon whilst my parents were away. We had sex right away. There was absolutely no talking. Afterwards, he immediately got up and stuck his head in a bowl of ice water! I felt I had been initiated. I also felt I must have done a pretty good job!

But as our relationship progressed, I started to feel anxious a lot of the time. I never knew what he was feeling or whether I was getting it 'right' or not. I somehow felt that if I could get him to like/love me, my needs would be met. I lived in a state of panic. I thought I could never relax or look slightly less than perfect, or he would leave. I tried to become the perfect girlfriend – a sexy boytoy, his armpiece, adorer. The few times I let more of the real me peek out, I experienced rejection the likes of which only existed on my 'worst fear' list. I went around in a hazy state of panic all the time.

Another woman, slightly older and divorced, describes very poignantly her feelings for the man she is having a relationship with:

Last weekend I saw him. We went boat riding, grocery shopping, and then to his home. He was fixing dinner for me. At this point, he grabbed me and kissed me. I was standing in the dark watching the lightning bugs out of the window when he came up behind me and put his arms around me and started caressing me, then turned me around a couple of times. Later when we were cooking dinner he put his arms around me again and really started kissing and caressing me. We were both very aroused. We turned

2

off dinner and had sex. Then we ate dinner and went to bed . . .

I asked him the next morning if he had any regrets and he said no, and we sat and drank coffee for an hour before I left. When I left, he kissed me again. This was Sunday morning and now it's Thursday night. I don't know if he's made up his mind that he can't handle being with me . . . or that he does care for me and is afraid of that. I'm beginning to feel less open and sharing.

PATTERNS YOU KNOW AND LOVE

What do these women have in common? They are saying they want to establish better relationships with the men they love, but that this is difficult. They are becoming tired of always being the ones who try so hard. Most women say that they feel they are giving men more emotional support than they are getting. Is this an individual problem? Why are so many women experiencing this? And why are the problems so hard to solve?

Listen as women pinpoint the real dynamics that are going on just beneath the surface of relationships – the problems that all too often plague us, but that have not been accurately named before.

Emotional withholding

One of the biggest problems in relationships, as women describe them, is a pattern we call emotional withholding on the part of men. In this pattern of behavior a person, while not being openly aggressive, can erect a fence around him or herself, keeping others at a distance. Men often use emotional withholding with women to maintain control in a relationship. It works like this: after the initial 'pursuit', when the man is very interested and attentive, he becomes ambivalent in his behavior, keeping the woman guessing about his feelings so that, before she knows it, she is spending a lot of time trying to figure out what is happening, why things are changing, why the relationship feels so

3

unsettling. She begins to try harder and harder to please him in an attempt to regain the original love or at least the sense of pursuit. This is a power trip for men that many are not even aware of using.

Emotional withholding takes several forms: the first is something we have probably all asked ourselves at some point:

'Why won't he talk to me?'

How often have you asked yourself, or heard one of your friends ask herself, one of these questions: 'Why won't he talk to me? Isn't he interested in what I think? If not, why is he with me, telling me he loves me?'

This silent withholding is frequently referred to as a 'lack of communication'. This is too imprecise: usually what is really going on is that the woman is trying to get the man to 'open up' and talk to her. It is not a two-way problem. Women say over and over again that they can share feelings, talk with their women friends, in a way that seems foreign to many men. They say that most men just do not open up in the same way that women do, and, especially, they don't really listen.

Waiting for a boyfriend or lover to open up and talk to you is frustrating – to say the least! Does what these women say sound familiar?

His refusal to really share himself with me drives me nuts. He just won't tell me what's going on. I always have to ask – and then the answers are minimal, as if there were a prize for the least amount of information he could disclose! You'll never know how many hours I've spent trying to figure out whether he *can't* talk to me or just *won't* talk to me.

He's often silent for hours when we are alone, which gets on my nerves. I would like him to talk more about feelings, reactions, problems, but he's just not inter-ested. He will only talk to me if he sees I'm desperate and start to cry . . .

4

Why is this happening? Don't men like talking to us? As one woman puts it, 'Aren't men interested in what the woman they are sleeping with has to say?'

Some men believe that 'Real Men' don't talk about feelings: that is for women. Real Men are 'rational', 'logical', 'scientific' and 'objective'. Despite all the discussion of the 'New Man', a lot of men still seem to panic when they come face to face with an emotion!

These wordless situations cause many women to wonder, 'Is it that he *can't* speak? Or that he *won't*?' While many men still buy into the 'stiff upper lip' world-view, others may just not *want* to share themselves. Most men are still taught to be afraid of looking even remotely 'wimpy' and, for many, talking about their feelings comes under this category.

Many men are even taught they are not supposed to be 'overly affected' by falling in love:

> When he leaned over to me and said, 'I love you,' it was a very big deal for me. When I smiled and tears welled up in my eyes, he said, 'God, you don't have to cry. I only said I loved you, nothing's different, it doesn't mean all that much! Jesus!'

'Is he really listening?'

Another way men typically express emotional withholding is by not listening:

> It is extraordinary to have a conversation with a man where you are pouring out something very important, something you may have been terrified to tell him or that you have been rehearsing for a long time in order to be as fair and as open as you can, and he just carries on with whatever he is doing. It has always been amazing to me that my boyfriend can sit in a room where I'm crying and not even look at me. I can't ever imagine doing the same to him.

> When we first started seeing each other, he would listen – or I thought he listened; maybe he was just enthralled with my presence. Later I noticed that when

5

I spoke, he would walk out of the room, look preoccupied, or totally neglect to answer me, even when I ended my thought with a question. That hurt.

My friends are genuinely interested in how I feel. We take turns talking and listening. Bill only wants a 'good listener'. Once I start to speak up and express opinions, he gets uncomfortable.

Sometimes women are surprised to find that after a man seems to be hearing them (at least, he *looks* like he is listening), later he has absolutely no recollection of anything that was said.

I tell him something and later he'll say, 'You never told me that.'

He does not hear what I am saying, he hears what he wants to hear.

One woman remembers a type of non-conversation she had in college:

Don was very kind and loving, but he didn't think that what women had to say was nearly as important as what men had to say. We would be hanging out at parties with his friends and some of mine, and the conversation would go something like this:

Guy 1: Yo, Donny, we nailed 'em. (Making a crude victory gesture and then putting Don in a half-nelson.)
Guy 2: Yeah, you didn't save that *too* brilliantly, did you Don?
Guy 1: Hey, Don, wanna beer? Candy, wanna beer? (Don kisses me on the cheek and asks me if I want a beer as he's walking away. I realize it doesn't matter what I say, I'm going to get a beer whether I want one or not. He assumes that I want what he wants.)
Guy 2: Candy, where'd you get that hat? (Tweaking the brim of my hat and pinching my cheek as one would a little baby.)

6

Guy 3: That's a weird hat. I don't mean weird, I've just never seen one before. (This is said without looking at me, sort of glancing around.)

Me: It's from the shop in Northampton that sells hats and gloves, you know ... (I look at him as I say this, but realize the question was not meant to be answered. Silence ...)

Guy 1: Hey, Don, you going to the Christmas party?

Don: Yeah, Candy and I are going.

Me: When is that? (No one answers me. I am now beginning to feel like jumping up and down and waving my hands in their faces so they take notice. Hello! H-E-L-L-O!)

Guy 2: I'm taking Melissa.

Guy 1: Melissa Capen?

Guy 2: Yeah ...

Guy 1: You're kidding! She's a bit of all right ... I gotta go ... I have Professor Valentine in the morning and we have an exam on the fundamentals of American Constitutional Law ...

Me: I took that last year ... He usually asks you questions on –

Guy 2: Sam told me it's all on the first section of the green text.

Me: Um, listen, I know what he asks ...

Guy 1 (to Guy 2): Really? Is he sure?

Me: Uh, I'm trying to tell you – (Small beads of sweat are now forming on my temples and upper lip.)

They all collectively decide that the conversation is over – and it is clear if they were asked to recollect it later, they probably would not remember that I was there.

Does this sound all too familiar? It has happened to most of us, and with 'nice' men, too. They *are* often nice men, but their attitudes to women are *not* nice: they just assume for the moment that women are totally redundant; their buddies are what matters.

One woman describes how this experience of not being heard makes her feel:

When he does this I feel all bound up inside, angry and trapped, as though I am wearing a mask and I can't get it off. He is looking at me but he doesn't see me. I am speaking coherently so why can't I be heard?

The message we get here is that these men are definitely not taking us seriously, and they sure as hell aren't interested in who we really are! They don't pick up on the subjects we initiate; one woman puts it like this:

Sure, we talk. As long as the subject is something he's interested in. If I want to bring something up that I'm interested in, forget it. Now I don't even try.

When your remarks are met by silence

Women say they are often greeted by silence when they offer their comments, even in small talk. We heard the following 'conversation' on the street:

Woman: That's a pretty dog.
Man: (No response.)
Woman: Well, it's got a pretty coat.
Man: (Silence.)

Women trying to live with men who are silent, or men who talk as little as they can and reveal even less, have a frustrating time of it. These men are not relating seriously to women. Under these circumstances, a woman may feel panicky and emotionally uncertain: 'He loved/wanted me in the beginning – what happened?' Then she thinks to herself, reasoning, 'This man is so different now from the way he was in the beginning. Who is the "real" man: the one I first met, or this one? It must be the one I first met, he's only behaving this way because there is some problem. Let me help him figure it out. As one who loves him, I shouldn't desert him just because things are difficult for the moment . . . We can work it out, together!'

But if a woman tells the man, 'You are behaving so differently, you're almost hostile – why?', she may very

8

well hear, 'But *I* haven't done anything wrong! I haven't even said anything!' Quite.

This 'insecure' feeling is a real and supremely logical response to a very real situation; that is, a relationship in which a man is withholding himself. The unnamed thing that is missing in relationships like these is real emotional expression from the man – a sharing of himself on a deeper level.

Sometimes when women try to talk about this emotional distance with a man, he turns around and says, 'Listen, get off my back. Your need for more communication is not realistic – it is part of your unresolved father thing!' While it is certainly true that many women's fathers didn't talk to them (or to their mother), or ask them how they felt and what they thought, this doesn't mean that women's desire for more communication is a neurosis! It *is* something unresolved, an unresolved 'male' problem in our society – a society which discourages men from 'talking like women do'. And this barrier to closeness is something most women desperately wish men would change. Women have changed over the past twenty years; so can men.

'Why is he so ambivalent?'

Another form of withholding often makes us ask ourselves, 'If he loves me, why is he so emotionally distant one day, so warm the next?' This form of withholding consists of a man expecting the woman always to be there with her love, but acting ambivalently about his own feelings: offering love erratically (just enough to keep her involved?). Often, he will say that he is 'confused' or 'can't make up his mind'.

One woman recounts the 'fun' experience she had during a so-called relationship with a man who kept stringing her along, offering love but never really clarifying his feelings for her:

He told me he was dating someone who was nice but not exciting – he said that '*it* just wasn't there' with her. I knew what he meant because I had felt like that before. Although we were very attracted to each other,

9

we agreed it would be better not to sleep together until he was free. He said it would be a matter of a few weeks. But when he was next in town, we spent the night together anyway, and he told me he loved me. Then I didn't hear from him for ten days. When he eventually called, I told him that no one could sleep with me and then just not bother to call! He apologized and I accepted it, because our night together had been *so* wonderful. And I *knew* how much he felt for me – at least I thought I did.

We slept together whenever we got the chance after that. He always said the most wonderful, romantic and passionate things to me, but the next day he would shuffle around and say he was still 'confused', 'unsure'. It was devastating. And each time it happened, I became more mistrustful and resentful. But I was hooked.

I started to fall really heavily. I truly believed that he had fallen for me too, but, when push came to shove, he always wanted to 'do the right thing' – that meant 'not hurting' this other woman and 'not hurting' me, either.

Each time he came to stay, I thought, 'This is it. Our night will be so wonderful that he'll wake up and say, "Christ, what the hell am I doing making this woman wait? Let me take the risk and find what I've always wanted here!"'

Then one day he told me that we couldn't see each other again 'in that way'. There was no way I wanted to be 'just good friends', so I told him I never wanted to see him again.

A few months later, he called to tell me he had finally finished his relationship with the other woman. I told him to fuck off. I found out much later that he was only 'free' from the relationship for about twenty-four hours. He's still seeing her today!

Guessing games: why does he play them?

What drives me crazy in a relationship is the not-knowing . . . not knowing if he really loves me, if he wants to marry me eventually, if he is just going along to see if we get along OK before he brings it up, or is he just taking me for a joy-ride for however long it lasts?

Who, when they listen to this woman, doesn't empathize – hearing either herself or many women she has known? How many hours have most of us spent trying to figure out by talking to friends what is going on in a man's mind?

That vague, uneasy state of not-knowing, the constant wondering what is going on, grows out of many men's pattern of withholding emotion and information from women. It is difficult to face the fact that withholding is a form of power and control commonly used by some men (including those we love) in relationships. It is painful to realize that someone could actually want to keep us in line by giving us just enough crumbs to keep us hanging on, but not enough to make a relationship flourish.

At first, the suspense of not-knowing in romance can be exciting, but after a few dates (particularly after the first sexual encounter), what some men may think is sexy, devil-may-care behavior quickly comes to infuse a relationship with insecurity, fear and distrust.

'No matter how many times it happens to you, it never seems to get easier,' one woman says, describing the famous first-he-acts-as-though-he's-crazy-about-you-and-then-he-doesn't-even-call act.

Ambiguous behavior on the part of men usually leads to intense soul-searching in women. We attempt to make things work by trying to figure him out, and then modifying our behavior accordingly. We fill the void that his silence or ambivalence creates by racking our brains: 'Did I do something? Did I not do something? Is my body good enough? Am I intelligent enough? What does he want me to be? Why won't he talk to me about it?' And if she then 'brings it up' (i.e. asks him), she is likely to be met with, 'What is all this about? You are manufacturing all this stuff in your head. Can't you relax?'

One woman describes how she would become so focused on the man's interests that she completely neglected her own:

When JJ said he would be in town in a week and we arranged to go out one night, I rearranged my life so that I could meet him. He didn't turn up and my whole week was wrecked. There I was, a responsible woman, and yet I was willing to juggle everything to accommodate him. I had let everything else slip just because I considered him to be more important. I was so hurt and angry when I never heard from him.

And another woman describes living through what has to be one of the most vague relationships on record:

I had just gone to my first football game, and, having been accustomed to dating men of small physiques with a penchant for looking as ill as they could in mimicry of their rock star idols, I was absolutely paralyzed with fascination by the hunks I saw there. They swore a lot and hung out with each other, and laughed at jokes and phrases I could never understand, but that I had a sneaking suspicion were at my expense. But all I wanted was for one of them to fall in love with me.

One night my friend and I went to a dorm party where a lot of animal noises and loud music were emanating from the windows. We went downstairs for a beer. I soon learned the most important thing to do when you arrived at one of these bashes was to look like you knew where you were going and what you were going there for. God forbid you should appear vulnerable or confused.

So I stood there and pretended to be talking to my friends about incredibly important, fascinating things and brilliant jokes, and they did the same. But we were really waiting for 'them' to notice us.

Then I was jabbed in the ribs by a not-so-popular-with-the-guys-but-wished-she-were senior who whispered in my ear: 'There's Al.'

He loomed in the doorway like a mack truck, power personified. And he knew it. He had a cut on his cheekbone from the game, wore an old tartan shirt, jeans that hung around his hips over a tiny butt, and a broad grin on his face. He was huge, male to the nth degree, totally involved with his friends and Totally Unavailable.

Nevertheless, Al and I began to have a sporadic sexual relationship. The night it first happened was at a party after a game. The whole basement floor was drenched in about four inches of warm beer. The 'men' were doing something called the 'beer slide', where they took a running leap at the floor and slid through the beer to the other side of the room. Very intelligent adult men, you understand.

Finally, only the girls with actual boyfriends were still there, so I started to leave. When he saw me getting my coat, Al shouted across the room, 'Yo, Susie, stay!' He walked over to me and picked me up. With one arm. Across his shoulder. Like a caveman. He carried me upstairs to someone else's room. As he walked in with me (giggling) over his shoulder, his friend looked up and saw us. There were no words spoken, only broad smiles and a punching-of-the-air gesture meant to symbolize victory. The friend left.

We went into bunk-beds for an episode that lasted approximately ten seconds. It was the single most physically unsatisfying sexual encounter I have ever had. It was so awful, but I was smiling, because I had 'got him'! It was like a badge of honor, like being admitted to an exclusive club. We went back down to the party and acted as though nothing had happened.

For the following weeks, nothing happened either. There were no phone calls, some flirting at parties, some (many) parties where he didn't even talk to me at all. Then, one night, we went back to his room and made love. He told me I was beautiful. Now I was on top of the world. He then invited me to his parents' house for a weekend. We got very drunk and had sex in a playing field in the dark with a transistor radio playing Bruce Springsteen. Then we returned to school. Again, nothing – no words.

By spring break, we met up at a party. We drank,

had fun with friends and went to the beach. I wrote his name in the sand. He pulled my chair next to his (I was on it) and asked me how I felt about him. It was all that 'I'm-not-going-to-tell-you-how-I-feel-first' stuff.

I wondered why he couldn't tell me first, and I talked around my real feelings, not using the word 'love', which is what I really, really felt. It was obvious that if I wanted to have this man, I couldn't say how I felt.

I wanted desperately to know how he was feeling about me, wanted so much for it to be love, but I felt it was safer to keep him guessing, just as he kept me guessing. I had taken that risk before in my life, and lived through being a yo-yo, so I felt too bounced around to be vulnerable with him.

He uttered something vague and then he fucked me. I never knew what it meant. I still don't. I never saw him again. It was all so confusing – the whole thing.

It's no wonder she felt confused!

DOUBLE MESSAGES FROM MEN

The double message is another of the undiagnosed patterns in relationships that become visible as women talk about what is going on. It is extremely important and helpful to pinpoint this behavior, as it relates to situations we encounter all the time.

The fact is, many men continually send out conflicting signals, as these women explain:

We were having a quick dinner out. But it got later and later, and I said, 'Darling, do you want to go on ahead home and do your work?' After a silence he said, 'Oh, no,' but with a tone of voice that meant, 'Yes.' I then said, 'Really, it's OK, I'll understand.' He sat immobile, like a martyr. Did he really prefer to be with me? I immediately became preoccupied with whether or not

I was pressuring him. Now, why couldn't he just have told me how he really felt?

I sat across from him at the bar last week and he said so many great things to me, such lovely things. He even looked like he was crazy for me, I could see it. But then I met a friend of his the next day and he said he had gone on holiday. Why didn't he tell me? So now I'm obsessed with this holiday and what he's doing. If he could just have been less sweet to me and less interested, I wouldn't have got so excited.

He did ask me once to marry him, but then he went out with my friend. He says he loves me and I shouldn't take a one-time fling with her seriously. Am I living in a fantasy? What does he really want?

We were out having a romantic evening. I was wearing a long skirt which was one of his favorites, and he told me I looked fantastic! But then he got up to go to the loo, and he didn't come back for half an hour. Finally, feeling humiliated and embarrassed at having been sitting there for so long, I went downstairs and found him talking to a waitress in a mini-skirt. He looked bashful, like he had been 'caught', and then came upstairs. He said, as if nothing was wrong, 'What a nice girl, and so attractive! Great legs,' and then he leaned over and kissed me on the cheek and said, 'I love you, you cute little thing. You look so adorable tonight, about twelve years old!' I felt horrible.

How would anyone react to these mixed signals? Women who love men who behave in this way logically feel 'insecure': the reality is that the position is unclear. Women are not irrationally 'needy' of 'reassurance'; too many men, whether they mean to or not, keep women guessing, through their own inner confusion and lack of straight-forward messages and actions.

What does all this mean? Although women are accused of being 'clingy', 'needy', 'overly focused on love' and 'obsessed with love', the reality is that many men behave in ways that show they *do* have very ambivalent feelings about loving a woman.

The logical progress of events in a situation like this is: first, the man displays very desirous behavior; the woman responds; then the man begins to be ambivalent; the woman tries to figure it out; he denies there's a problem; and she starts to question her own perceptions. Whose 'reality' is right? If she pursues it, still feeling uncertain, he may accuse her of 'nagging': 'Let it alone, won't you?' Now she really feels bad.

After all this, it's no wonder that hundreds of women every day grab at anything that will cover up the frustration and worry: pills, chocolate, cigarettes, whatever.

Women trying to have a relationship with a man are often thrown into a state of anxiety and end up spending an inordinate amount of time trying to decipher his behavior. This can be very nerve-racking and debilitating. How can you maintain a positive attitude and your self-esteem under these circumstances?

Although we can see that *logically* all these double messages are the reason for our uneasiness, who can help but hear a small inner voice that says, 'He must be a little bit right. I *am* very insecure. Maybe I am hysterical and emotionally dependent! I had better change or I will drive him away. I must stop clinging and become less selfish, try harder to be more as he wants me to be.' The awful part of this last thought is that we have denied the man's part in this set-up – after all, he did have something to do with the situation!

Women deserve more direct communication from men. Why play games?

'Why do I feel lonely and insecure, even when he's telling me he loves me?'

It is remarkable how many women say they have felt that, even while a man is telling them he loves them, he is also telling them (indirectly) what is wrong with them.

One woman remembers a particularly infuriating event in her life:

After the first night we had sex, Eddie put his arms around me, sort of feeling my waist and hips. Then he walked away and sat down. I was feeling wonderful; having been celibate for about nine months, his touch had felt exquisite, and I really liked him. He then asked me if I was the weight that I wanted to be. I was a little taken aback but said, 'Yes.' He just said, 'Oh,' and went into the bathroom.

I sat there feeling devastated. I had just shared my bed with this man, and he was already judging my body, giving no reassurance or appreciation. When he came out, I asked him why. He said, 'Well, you could lose a few pounds.' When he saw my face fall, he said, 'Don't look so upset. After all, *you* asked.' Oh, I see. It was *my* fault. I wasn't perfect, and it was my problem if I couldn't face the truth. Because we had slept together he apparently had every right to let me know how I could 'improve' myself. And if the information bothered me so much, then I had only myself to blame because *I* had asked.

Many women live in the midst of other forms of ambiguity:

Sometimes he seems to love me and like me, other times he doesn't, or he acts cold and distracted. He refuses to talk about our future, even though we have been going out for ten months – or about whether we have a future. He just changes the subject if I bring it up. I don't know what to do or think. I really like him, so I'll try to stick it out. But I feel out of touch and out of control a lot of the time.

The problem is that first he says he's vulnerable and in love, then later he denies it or doesn't act like it, acts cold. I ask myself, 'Is the goal this man at any cost?' It's almost as if someone is egging me on into the deep end of the pool – and when I get there (with my emotions) and really fall in love, trust him, he says, 'What? Why me?'

He tells me he loves me, but he is so changeable, makes and breaks dates at the last minute, and things like that. So I'm doing something that I really feel horrible about. I call his number to see if he's home when he says he'll be. If he doesn't answer, I go to the club we usually go to and pretend I'm out for the evening with friends, then see if he's there. If he's not, I look for his friends and try to find out (surreptitiously) where he is. On the other hand, if when I call, he is at his flat, I just hang up and tell myself I shouldn't be so silly.

Do these men love these women? Maybe yes, maybe no. Do the men themselves know? Their confusion, withholding of information and double messages can lead to our spending large amounts of time wondering, trying to figure it all out.

After all, even if men do or say contradictory things, they can't be irrational, can they? They must know which one they mean, mustn't they? We must be the ones who can't 'get it' – right?

What is the answer to all this? Keep reading!

MEN AS 'STARS'

When I was three or four, my mother was already teaching me to *see* dust and other people's feelings ('Don't bother your father, he's tired').

Although I find that I'm funny, sarcastic and energetic when in mixed groups, 'the life of the party' – when my boyfriend's there . . . boom. I'm very quiet. Almost like I don't want to steal his 'spotlight'.

We have heard a lot about the New Man, but how many of us have genuinely equal relationships?

I guess on paper you would say we were equal, but that's a load of crap in reality. Any big decisions, including ones that directly affect me, are made without my input.

18

We live in a very small apartment (one room), on a noisy street. My boyfriend works nights, so it's really important that he gets enough rest, what with the traffic sounds and me trying to keep the baby quiet. Anyway, I try to be really careful about that, I'm always considering him and his need for rest – I unplug the phone and don't watch TV. But when I've put in a twelve-hour day, he doesn't think twice about waking me up for a little sex whenever he feels horny. If I don't act thrilled to be woken up (if I seem annoyed), he gets pissed off and sulks. It's sort of like his schedule and needs are the first thing we *both* should think about, and mine are second.

If I was on the phone to one of my customers, he would want me to drop the customer so I could talk to him. If I was in a meeting, he would leave messages for me. I had a territory with several hundred customers and I had to spend a lot of time in the field. If he called me when I was out, when I returned his call he would ask me where I had been, who I was with, etc. I felt like I was a little kid checking in with my Dad.

So many men seem to assume that their opinions and ideas are more important than women's, and that their own needs come first. Now, of course, many so-called New Men would deny this, express surprise at the accusation or react more angrily.

But the fact is, most women are still in the unfair position of having to struggle against men's assumptions that *their* view of reality is the *correct* view – no dialogue necessary:

What we do is always his decision – whether we go out to eat in the first place, then whether we have dinner alone or with friends, when he calls me, and so on.

One woman feels her relationship slipping away because of this:

At first it was just like in the movies. We couldn't get enough of each other, body and mind. Then I started to want to talk more, to work things out before they got to be really big problems. But he always changed the subject as soon as I started to explain. He would say he was going to go work out, hang out with some friends, go fishing. It always happened to be right after I had brought something up. It got to the point where I would sit in the window of our apartment and watch him drive away and look down at the ring on my finger and wonder, 'What is happening? How did it get like this? It wasn't always like this, was it?'

This problem has existed for a long time. Most of our homes were controlled, either overtly or covertly, by the 'head' of the household, and what our fathers said was gospel. Boys who grow up like this then tend to perpetuate this belief system in their own lives, forming the same patterns with women they love/live with. These left-over assumptions are what women today find themselves trying so hard to end.

Many women tell poignant stories of this dynamic in their own childhood:

When I got home from school in the afternoons, my mother and I would talk about what had happened that day, fix something in the kitchen, hang out. When we heard the car pull in the drive, that meant my father was home from work, and the tone would change. My mother would become distant, and prepare to greet him. The rest of the evening, she and I would remain distant, not really talking to one another, as if somehow that would be intrusive to him, would offend his sense of being given most of the attention. It was never anything explicit, just a feeling in the air.

I learned from my mother that the proper attitude toward my father was to defer to him and give his opinions the most time and attention.

My father would criticize me for everything, from little things to big things. When he decided that a particular night was going to be one when he 'taught us something', my sisters and I knew we were in for a long one. We weren't allowed to express ourselves at all, just had to sit there and take the criticism, take the endless lectures and the insistence that if we didn't live life *his* way, we would end up where we belonged – hussies on the street corner. He always managed to mention sex and the 'looseness of women' every time. If I ever tried to talk back to him, or even just simply to express my own point of view, I would get blasted from here to the moon. I learned it wasn't worth it, but I still tried now and then. I just couldn't stand the pain of my own silence.

Do men define 'reality'?

Again and again, women describe men's assumptions that they are right, and have the right to criticize women's opinions and actions:

> When we have a disagreement, he belittles me into being quiet. He has this need to always be right, which certainly does not solve anything.

> He interrupted me on the phone to tell me I was crazy and stupid to suggest what I was saying.

When you are in this kind of relationship you may find that you apologize when you don't really want to, just to keep the peace. This practice is painful and, ultimately, can be dangerous. Having to deny our feelings and who we are – to ignore how we *really* feel – is mind-boggling on a long-term basis.

One woman describes a typical occasion:

> I was wearing a lovely summer dress that he hadn't seen before. It had embroidery on the front, with tiny little holes in the stitching. It was backless so I could not wear a bra with it. He said, 'Jesus, I can see your nipples through those holes. I can't believe you are wearing that out!' I said I thought he would like it, that

no one else could see. I thought it was romantic. He was furious. When we got home, I had to spend an hour apologizing for embarrassing him in public and for wearing such a stupid fucking dress.

Women as co-stars

Generally, men live their lives as though they were starring in them . . . many men will never take the time and effort to find out what's inside their mates. Co-stars.

One of the areas that is most telling for female/male relationships is who is waiting for whom. For instance, are you always the one who is waiting for him, wondering when he'll arrive? While you might not mind waiting if you know *when* he will arrive, just waiting indefinitely means that he is the one in control.

In other words, as 'stars', men set the agenda of emotional 'reality' in the relationship – sometimes psychologically bullying a woman into 'accepting' his terms, even though inside she may not agree. But if she wants him, she may have to accept his definition of things ('reality') thus damaging herself, having to internalize the idea that *her* perception of reality is slightly 'crazy', 'neurotic', or at least 'wrong'.

In relationships there should be mutual discussion of situations, to arrive at a consensus. But most men are not yet ready to really 'hear' women to this extent; they assume without really thinking that their view of reality and the relationship is right.

These powerful unacknowledged dynamics can have a pernicious effect on a relationship, as one woman describes:

Ed truly believed that all our problems were my fault, and was so convincing that my own perception of what was really going on became distorted beyond belief. As the relationship 'grew', I became trapped in a downward spiral, being unable to express my doubts or problems – I censored *myself* after a while, assuming the problems were mine and I should 'work on myself' to figure them out.

By acting as if their needs are important and ours are not, their version of reality is real and ours is not, then telling us when we try to point this out and get a dialogue going that we are 'whining' and 'insecure', men are practising a form of double-speak (and psychological abuse). They are illogically putting us down for our very logical reaction to tyrannical behavior.

A question for the 1990s

Are women obsessed with love? The common theory is that if women would only stop loving 'too much' (in effect, be more like men), they would find that they are happier and wouldn't have so many problems with love.

But if women are forced to relegate love to second or third position in their lives, and to become as competitive as Real Men – more male than men! – won't everyone be the loser? Isn't the solution for men to become more loving and nurturing, to take on some of women's traditional characteristics?

Women's interest in and discussion of love and personal relationships – so often ridiculed – is important. What women are struggling with is one of the most important issues of our times: how to love, how to restore feeling and emotion to life, and how not to be trashed by those who would take advantage of them, of their abilities to nurture and give.

Instead of women loving less, why can't men love more, be more emotionally supportive and involved? Why must it always be *women* who are asked to change?

BITCHY COMMENTS FROM MEN

He's always criticizing me. Then he says, 'What's the matter? Can't you take it?'

Women's daily lives are 'enhanced' by the sort of casual criticism this woman describes:

> When I didn't wash my hair one evening, the first thing my boyfriend said to me was, 'Oh, didn't you wash your hair today, hon? Well, don't worry, it looks fine anyway,' in this kind of fake sweet voice. Or another time, I wore sexy lingerie I thought he'd like and he said, 'What's the matter, couldn't you afford more expensive stuff? That looks sleazy.' Or the other day when I went out to a movie with my friends, he found out when it was over, decided what time I 'should' get home, then yelled at me for 'hanging out with the girls all night'! I knew he was being ridiculous, but I did hesitate about going out with them again this week.

This kind of pattern works like intimidation. The next time, we try to modify our behavior, as this woman describes:

> With this guy I starve myself to look thin, rush home from work to make the house look really welcoming, try everything to make him happy. My reward? The other day he said to me, 'You're so perfect, you're becoming a real drag. Why can't you be more feminine?' Now I find myself trying to figure out how to do *that*.

Sometimes if a woman then complains or cries at the criticism, or asks for clarification, the man will say, 'Oh, why are you so sensitive? I was only teasing you!' (Sometimes adding, 'You know I love you!') But these kinds of side-swipes and unproductive criticism are similar to the double messages women talked about earlier; women have several layers of meaning to deal with, leading them to become preoccupied, trying to figure out what they are. They hope that straightening out the 'problems' will lead to the original love in the relationship returning.

The 'fun' of language

Some forms of criticism are so standard that they are built into the language – you know, those good old clichés which are usually reserved just for women!

Have you ever had any of these leveled at you? Have you ever been told you are:

pushy, demanding, complaining, neurotic, bitchy, self-indulgent, hysterical, screaming, irrational, petty, needing reassurance, overly emotional, too sensitive, babyish, pathetic, crazy, in need of help, insane, erratic, moody, at it again, nagging, difficult?

Have you ever heard *men* called any of these things?

Unfortunately, many men who do love women still plug into this kind of language when they are irritated or upset; these words will just creep into the conversation. They may also be used by strangers, just 'in passing'. To challenge them, under the circumstances, would seem to be over-reacting. But it would be very understandable if a woman did react angrily at being called names that, given their history and meaning, are used to put women down or 'keep them in their place'.

While we may shrug off these words in general, when someone we love starts using them, it is difficult not to be shaken by self-doubt. If, by chance, we then turn to that same person for 'reassurance', we stand a good chance of being put down again! This becomes a self-fulfilling horror show, for there is no end to what we can blame ourselves for when someone we love keeps telling us what is wrong with us.

Don't be shut up by stereotypes!

Lots of women describe the names men call them:

When my friends and I try to make plans with our boyfriends, ask when they will be back and so on, they call us things like 'nags', 'policemen', 'ball-and-chains'. One guy, when he was out with his mates, with his girlfriend waiting at home, even called her 'the terminator'.

These labels can either be enraging or hysterically funny, depending on one's mood. It goes without saying that few women *want* to act as killjoys or be labelled as such. Women make 'rules' or ask questions when the men in their lives show little consideration: the 'rules' and questions are women's attempt to make the relationship work by drawing the line *somewhere*, before they get so angry that they just walk out.

The cowardly critic

Another form of hostility is more insidious; it is the critic who gives you such heavily veiled criticism that you end up thinking you are crazy. And he supports that belief, saying, 'I treat you so well – you must be paranoid.'

This pattern of veiled criticism, being put down indirectly, and thus attacked indirectly, was the thread running through one woman's long relationship:

After going out with Larry for about nine months – lots of parties and all – I started to need more closeness. There was virtually no intimacy, we were just the party pair. I began trying to be more romantic, to cook lovely dinners, have whole evenings when we stayed in bed, spent time together. But it was like swimming upstream. I tried really hard, but it got lonelier and lonelier. On the other hand he was always around, wanting to go out with me, so I thought he must care.

Eventually I started crying every morning, *every day*, because our 'intimacy' the night before left me feeling so hollow. I tried to tell him but we would fight again because he hated me crying. He called my tears 'morning sickness' and left it at that.

I decided to make one last stab at getting things to be different. A couple from France were visiting, and we planned a big party. I got dressed up in a smashing new outfit, then made my entrance. As usual, he said nothing. But when the French woman walked out of her bedroom to join us, he said, watching her every move, 'She looks incredible! French women have such style, don't you think?' He must have known how this made me feel, the brilliant sadist that he was. And what a great way to keep me in my place!

Many women describe feeling very lonely in their relationships – *more* lonely than if they were on their own:

During the last relationship I had with a man I spent moments so lonely I sometimes wondered if everyone else had disappeared off the face of the earth.

I'm so glad to have finally divorced him and started my life again because I felt so incredibly alone when we were married. Isolated. Ignored. Now I can give more attention to my son and have fun and experience life without the fear that I'm going to be criticized or 'iced' – my husband was a genius at being so cold when he didn't want to talk that you could swear you were in Siberia.

Being constantly put down, *especially* indirectly, plus having your thoughts and feelings ignored ('unheard') or flatly dismissed as 'ridiculous' by the one who says he loves you, is confusing to say the least. How on earth do you match the feelings we associate with the word 'love' with this kind of behavior?

Criticism is normal, of course. Throughout any relationship, people who love one another criticize each other – hopefully with tenderness and a constructive aim. But what women here are describing is different: a pattern of constant, indirect criticism, being put down as part of a daily routine, which amounts to emotional battering. We have seen the clichéd insults that are such a part of everyday language – language which men frequently take for granted as OK. This problem is compounded by the fact that, since society tells men they are the natural 'stars' of relationships, they often assume they have the right to 'set the standards' for our behavior *and* inform us when we do not meet these standards – to tell us what is 'wrong' with us.

When this emotional battering becomes a way of life in a relationship, it is difficult to make a man stop and realize that his assumptions and premises are bigoted – and so persuade him to rethink and change them before the relationship is ruined.

SABOTAGE

Some women say their relationships contain incidents in which their partner forgets things that matter, or seems to trivialize them:

My husband would make my life harder, but never in ways I could really 'catch' him, so he always looked like a 'good guy'. For example, I was hosting a barbecue for about forty of my colleagues – it was an important occasion for me. While I was out of the house, one colleague phoned to inquire whether he still needed to bring his extra skewers – my husband said 'no', leaving me without an adequate number to serve everybody. To this day, I don't know whether he really didn't know I was short (but why didn't he tell the man to bring them anyway, if he wasn't sure?) or if it was some subtle way of getting back at me for being so 'overly preoccupied' with 'fussing' over my 'party'.

It was my twenty-ninth birthday and I was feeling good. I went home from work and got a bouquet from my Mum and phone calls from my friends, but none from my boyfriend. I was disappointed, but I hoped he would make up for it later.

We planned to meet at my favorite restaurant, my boyfriend and about ten other friends. He didn't really like my friends, (and they didn't like him much either), but I thought it would probably be OK just for tonight, since it was my birthday and he couldn't possibly be rude to them and humiliate me.

I got to the restaurant early and waited at the bar. My

friends started arriving, with tulips and little presents. It was so sweet, and I felt so happy to be cared for.

Then he walked in, no smile or anything. He thrust an old plastic bag into my hand. I opened it and inside was a toy for three to four year olds. You pull a little string and it tells you how to cross the street or to say thank you. I couldn't believe it. I looked up at my best friend and I saw her seething. This was not funny, it was like him saying, 'I'll give you what I want, when I want, and if you don't like it, tough.' It was like, 'Let's see how much humiliation you can take and still be gracious.'

Throughout dinner he ignored me or was rude and insulting, so the whole table was silenced. More friends arrived, and at this point I was embarassed at how nice they were being to me because it showed how lousy *he* was being. I was so ashamed.

Finally, I had to get up from the table because I felt unable to hold back my tears. I was so hurt. But I dared not let him see, because God knows what he would have said *then*. My girlfriend laid into him, and when he refused to talk with her about how upset I was, they all left. They couldn't stand it any more, and I don't blame them.

Then at his house he started on me, yelling at me about my friends, what was wrong with them, how shitty I was to be so upset, what's the matter with me, blah, blah, blah. I just sat there and cried. How could I explain to him when he was so removed from what had *actually* happened?

In the end, I just kept saying over and over, 'It's my birthday, how could you do this? It's my birthday . . . ' and walked out.

Living in an emotionally aggressive atmosphere

One of the most common, yet unnamed, causes of fights in relationships is emotional battering or emotional violence. The atmosphere these attitudes create, built as they are into the language about women – and into 'trivial' everyday behavior towards women – forms the background against which most relationships are lived. This frame of reference can create so much tension, defensiveness and discomfort that many single women even try to avoid getting involved in new relationships.

CHANGING THE EMOTIONAL CONTRACT

The intricate and assumed psychological patterns taught to women and men form a kind of 'emotional contract' in which the woman is expected to nurture the man, take care of his emotional needs, but not vice versa. This interaction has been left out of nearly all the standard analyses of love relationships. The typical pattern is this: a man will withhold equal emotional openness from a woman, distance himself emotionally (whoever is less vulnerable has more power . . .), trivialize her and not listen to her, *then* turn to her looking for love, affection and understanding ('A woman should be there for a man').

How should a woman react to someone who is frequently emotionally distant and inaccessible, even ridiculing her or not listening, yet who then turns to her expecting love and affection, saying he loves her?

Women have been criticized in recent years for being 'too loving', too giving, too nurturing, or obsessed with 'romance'. The theory has been that women rely too much on love for their fulfillment in life, that as women we 'cling', because we are brought up to be psychologically dependent, and even that we are 'crippled' psychologically. We are told that if only women would give up behaving in this manner and stop loving 'too much' (in effect, think more like men), we would find that we would be happier and have fewer problems with love. But this leaves out the other participants in the drama: men.

Clearly, the problems in a relationships have as much to do with men as with women. However, an analysis of men's behavior is almost never carried out, and it is pointedly left out of most discussions of 'female psychology', as if female psychology existed in a void. And yet, if men are taught in all kinds of ways that they are superior,

more privileged, or 'different' from women, this must
surely affect how they behave towards women (including
those they truly love) in their relationships.

We have seen that the feelings of insecurity women may
have are usually part of a complex interaction: if a man
insists on withholding his feelings, this puts the burden on
the woman to do most of the 'emotional housework', to
keep the channels of communication open. By doing this,
women are making relationships possible. How ironic
then, to put women down for this! How rude to berate
women for being 'too demanding' and 'always wanting to
talk'.

There is another irony here: while women are labelled as
needing to talk and communicate more, most men are
already getting this kind of attention from women, so they
do not have to ask for it (or be seen to 'need' it). Isn't it
interesting to note that most men do not turn to other men
to fulfill their emotional needs? In the *Hite Report on Male
Sexuality* the great majority of married men said that their
best friends were their wives. However, in *Women and Love*
most married women, although they generally said they
loved their husbands, also said that if *they* want to talk, they
turn to their best friends: women.

In short, the reality behind many of these situations is not
that women are neurotic, some kind of Freudian shadow-
women who live their lives in agonies of insecurity. The
truth is that the dynamics many men set in motion, by
caustic or condescending remarks, make it necessary for
women to question what is going on: why the man is saying
these things and whether they really want to be in the
relationship. It is a pity that so many of the intricate feelings
we happily share with other women are blocked by men;
we cannot talk as easily with them because they feel
uncomfortable.

What women are saying is that they simply wish men
would drop their out-dated ideas about themselves and
about women, stop being afraid of being seen as 'weak' if
they *really* love, and start trying to empathize and think of
women as emotional equals. Most women want men to

turn over a new leaf and learn to love with emotional equality – without fear.

EMOTIONAL VIOLENCE: A DEFINITION

What we have been seeing, in its many guises, is something we can now name: emotional violence. Emotional violence – or emotional battering, aggression and harassment – are so prevalent and all-pervasive in our society, such a part of our daily lives, that they are generally accepted as 'reality'; we are told it is 'human nature', 'men are like that'.

Emotional violence is a large-scale social problem, not a biologically determined 'way we are'. However, there is no widespread recognition that the dynamics of love relationships reflect women's inequality in society. We are told that men and women become equal in 'love'. Thus the problems in a relationship caused by women's second-class status are swept under the carpet, called 'women's problems' (women are 'neurotic', always 'moaning and complaining'), and so 'individualized' away. Emotional violence is also covered up by doctors over-prescribing tranquilizers to women and by advice books telling women how to 'live with it'.

This negative Freudian view of women, as deserving their second-class status has suffused much of twentieth-century art, literature and politics. In this book we are breaking with that tradition and presenting a new analysis of what is going on.

The inequality of the emotional contract – what is expected of men vs. what is expected of women – is so ordinary, it is accepted as 'the way things are', 'the way things have always been', and 'the way things will always be'. But things don't have to be this way.

Some may say that pointing out men's tendency towards emotional harassment of women is 'hostile' and 'inaccurate'. However, if one thinks that only ten years ago the statistics on physical battering became clear, and now it has been shown that over 85 per cent of cases of spouse abuse are carried out by men, it cannot be surprising that *emotional* battering, violence and aggression against women are part of a way of life in our society. It is obvious that a climate of emotional abuse will be more prevalent than its extreme form, physical abuse.

Although most women feel that something is not quite right in the emotional balance of their relationships, that somehow there is a built-in power imbalance, that men say more 'mean' things to women during fights, for example, than women do – this has been difficult to state, until now. Women were called 'paranoid' if they said they thought something unfair was going on. And many of us did not consciously label the 'something wrong' as the form of psychological aggression or abuse it is, because, as we have seen, society encourages women to blame themselves, just as it encourages men to blame women. As a comedian once said, 'My boyfriend and I had two things in common: we both loved him and hated me.'

This general atmosphere – that it is the woman's fault if things go wrong, she is the 'nag', or she is 'manipulative' or 'impossible to live with' (the famous wife jokes) – makes many of us constantly question our own perception of what is really going on. Sometimes we even think (or are told) we must be 'crazy' to get so upset. But, the reality is that our society's code of behavior reinforces men's condescending attitudes, and creates major problems for women in love relationships.

In fact, the unequal emotional contract is the major problem in most love relationships – women and men are, in a way, 'star-crossed lovers' from birth. The sooner this is acknowledged, the sooner personal relationships will improve. Surely, working together, we can put an end to these unnatural prejudices, and learn to enjoy our lives and our love for one another with far less heartache and a lot more happiness.

A new emotional contract

Love – does it have to be so difficult? Have we been much too negative so far in this book? Well, we bet you have recognized at least one or two quirky problems you have had.

First, we want to say that none of these blastedly difficult pretzel-shaped love affair problems are *our* fault. It's not *our* fault that men are still growing up with images of Rambo and the Marlboro man, the idealized 'loner'. It's not our fault that so many men feel paralyzed with fear in the face of emotions. So don't blame us!

We're here to help straighten out this mess. Hopefully, after this new and insightful analysis, you won't have to be emotionally on the defensive any more.

There is a real conflict between who we are, who we have become as women in the late twentieth century, and the out-dated demands many men still put on us.

It's time to revise relationships so that they are more emotionally equal, more fun – happier. Time to understand and change what is really going on, so that love can last.

—2—

The New Sexuality

Sex. Are women in the 1990s going to enjoy sex more than ever before, or are they tired of it after the problematic 1980s? What about monogamy? Have things changed in some fundamental way for women?

CAN THE DOUBLE STANDARD STILL BE AROUND?

Having sex shifts the power thing: when you meet the next night, why is it. . . ? You are no longer just two equals having dinner.

Does the double standard really still exist? What about the New Man? Aren't most men today, the New Men, thinking for themselves, going beyond the old stereotype that men must 'score' (because this is really masculine) but that any woman who will have sex with them is a bit of a slut?

Believe it or not, this ridiculous attitude is still around. Most women say that after they have had sex with a man, there is a basic change in the relationship. Before, the woman was the 'desired'; after, she often feels as though she's the 'had'!

Of course, not all men are like this, but this thinking is still common, even among teenagers.

Lines men love to use – still!

Some of the current lines going around range from amazing, hilarious or insulting to just plain stupid. See if there are any here you have heard and wish you hadn't!

You aren't going to sleep with me? Why did you bother dressing up in all that please-fuck-me clothing then?

It's the will of God.

But I paid for your dinner!

If we sleep together we can get rid of this sexual tension in our friendship.

Do you have your diaphragm in?

I'm twenty. I can't believe I'm twenty and have never gotten laid.

My balls hurt.

If you get hit by a truck tomorrow, you may die without ever having slept with the best.

Are you gay or something?

You say you don't, but I know you *really* want to.

Do you want to get a pizza and then fuck? (She slaps him.) What's the matter, you don't like pizza?

Want to dance? No? Well, I guess a blow job's out of the question.

If you don't, I'll tell everyone that you did.

I know we only just met, but I think I love you.

And, finally, the classic:

I'll still respect you in the morning!

Snappy retorts

Women have suggested some perfect comebacks. In response to these unappealing come-ons, try saying:

36

Don't you remember me? I'm the one who called you pencil-dick.

Yeah, but can my mother come too?

No, but I'll pay you to go away.

I like girls.

I have a feeling you'd disappoint me.

Do you have a great deal of money? I'm pregnant and looking for someone to slap a paternity suit on.

Him: Can I buy you a drink?
Her: No, but I'll take the cash.

How soon should you have sex?

The period of starting a new relationship – or having sex to find out if it is a relationship – is one of the most exciting yet agonizing times for women. The pressure to settle down and be monogamous in the 1980s, and the fear of AIDS, were supposed to take the pressure off women to have sex at the drop of a hat. But this is not what most women are experiencing. They say that many men still expect sex on the first date:

When I first went out with him, we kissed and fooled around and even though I was excited, I wanted to wait for a while before we had sex, just to feel good about it. But he didn't. He was shocked when I insisted.

We had sex the first time we went out. It was in the heat of the moment. The next morning I felt anxious – I wondered whether he was going to call me again. He didn't. I have learned you can't give it all away too soon if you want him to come back for more. I like to have time to get worked up about somebody, over a couple of weeks, so that when we do it, we are both really excited.

There is also the problem of men sometimes ridiculing women for any idea that the sex they just had might be more than recreational:

> After the first time we made love, he said, 'Let's not get serious.'

> We lay there after this incredible sex and he turned to me, looking so beautiful, and said, 'Listen, babe, you seem to be taking this to heart. Really serious. Well, I'm not. I mean, I thought we could just have some fun and there would be no demands.'

> The sex was so romantic, he was really passionate and loving, even though I didn't know him very well. I knew I could really fall for this one. Then afterwards, he just got up and slipped on his jeans and turned on the TV. Then he tossed me my clothes and said, 'You'd better get up, my friend's coming over.' I knew then that I had been feeling this great passion all by myself.

These women point out that *before* they slept with him, the man didn't state any of these limitations or preconditions. On the contrary, most men do everything to look sincere and sweet and worth having sex with.

So women spend a good deal of time and energy worrying about when to have sex, much more time than men need to invest. Women try to figure out whether they 'should' or 'shouldn't' have sex by trying to decipher men's behavior beforehand. Women still have to watch out for their 'reputations' even after all the rhetoric of the 'sexual revolution' has supposedly ended the double standard. The double standard is alive and well, and most men have not yet begun to really question their own assumptions about it.

When a woman feels that if she doesn't sleep with a man relatively quickly he may never call her again, but if she does sleep with him he may not take her seriously, she is put in a very strange and insulting position.

So many times I've dated men who couldn't do enough for me before we slept together. They would kiss the ground I walked on! Then we would sleep together and suddenly they hardly bothered to call.

I used to flirt with this bartender who was really handsome. Everybody wanted him, but he wanted me. I used to fantasize how he was aching for me. Then one night we did it in the ladies' room – it was great. But then he just zipped his pants up and went back to work! I felt powerless, like the thing that gave me my power, my 'booty', had been given to him and now he wasn't interested any more.

It would be so great to know that when I flirt with a guy, he is turned on, but not in a way that demeans me – just in a sexy way. And that, if we have sex, we can both be sure that we are going to be nice to each other after, no matter what, even if we only do it once and one of us decides that it is not right for us, whatever the reason. People should be nice about it.

It is so infuriating when men behave as if they don't care after the event – when *before* we had sex they were sweet and sensitive! Do they think I'm impressed? No! I just think they are jerks. But how can I know how they will act *after* sex until I *have* sex?

The general idea goes something like this: 'If we have sex, it doesn't mean anything and shouldn't lead you to "expect" anything. So I might call you again and I might not, but let's not worry about that now, let the future happen when it happens. If you can't, there's something wrong with you!'
The implicit 'rule' is 'stay casual, no strings attached'. But, although many women *do* enjoy casual sex at some times in their lives, most say that they really prefer sex as part of stronger feelings, part of a friendship or relationship – even if it is a one-night stand. And they especially do not want to be disrespected afterwards.
Why are men allowed any and all means of expressing themselves sexually – with feelings, without feelings, and

as often as they like – while women are not supposed to? And why do people still accept (and even encourage) men to get ego boosts by fucking as many women as possible, meanwhile feeling free to look down on women if they are 'too sexual'. You *still* hear, 'It's OK to *fuck* a woman like that [who really turns you on] but not *marry* her!'

In this dating scenario the man is defining everything on his terms. He is supposed to decide if he wants to see the woman again. And he supposedly decides whether he will give her the status of 'a woman to be taken seriously', 'a woman to be used for sex', or 'a woman to be dropped'. This is a nasty form of sexism – a preconceived set of values which is very difficult to fight against.

Should men be less 'free' or should women be more 'free'?

Does 'sexual equality' mean women should be more 'free', like men? Or does it mean men learning some of women's sensitivity to feelings, not pushing for sex at the drop of a hat but taking on some of women's values about sex?

Many men still believe in the three-date rule: if a man has taken a woman out three times and she does not then 'give in' and allow him to sleep with her, he should move on to the next 'conquest'. However, women say that even if they *do* have sex by the third date, the man will *still* move on – because now he has 'had' her, so why stay!

Try asking men you know whether they believe in the double standard. Most of them will probably say they don't. But then try this: ask them whether a woman they were thinking of marrying would still be as appealing if they discovered she had slept with, say, thirty men that year. Ten to one they will say she would not. Then ask them what they would think of a male friend who had had the same number of partners in the same amount of time. They will no doubt admit they admire him.

If men are asked to choose between being less promiscuous or giving women the same sexual freedom as they have, more often than not men choose the latter. However, see how many of them would consider marrying one of those women!

The sexual politics of the one-night stand

The one-night stand is still going strong, as one woman confirms:

> My sex life is a joke. The men who are interested in me seem to be only interested in something very casual, or a one-night stand. I come off feeling worse than if I had had no sex at all. To say, 'I feel so cheap,' sounds silly, but that's exactly how I feel.

Another woman tells how she took revenge on a man who had used her to score a one-night stand:

> I went out with Sam twice about two months ago. The reason I went out with him in the first place was he kept telling me how beautiful I was, and I was a real sucker for it. 'Oh, you have such beautiful legs, such beautiful eyes . . . ' I should have known.
>
> The first time, I didn't sleep with him. But the second night I stupidly did, and he never called me again.
>
> Then one day I ran into him on the street, and, like an idiot, invited him to a party I was giving. I didn't tell anyone except my best friend I'd invited him – because I knew everybody would pounce on me for being a masochist. I hoped he wouldn't show up, so nobody would ever know I'd broken down and invited him. But he showed up, and I ignored him. Then we were in the kitchen and he tried to kiss me. I looked at him and said, 'Sam, why on earth would I want to kiss you? The last time I slept with you, you didn't even call me again. So why would I want to do that?' And he said, 'You're making me feel guilty!'
>
> So anyway, after the party, we went with some people to a coffee shop and he kept touching me and stuff, acting like I was his date. When we all left, he started kissing me on the street. I was real uninterested, but he said to me anyway, 'Do you want to make love now?' This guy is so persistent – if you say no, he

just asks you again! Ten times, until he sort of wears you down – that is what happened last time. And I said, 'Of course not. For what? You know how I feel, I've already told you. This is ridiculous.' He just ignored that and said, 'Don't you want to come to my place?' I said, '*No!*' He then said, 'Can I walk you upstairs?' (to my apartment).

I thought to myself, 'If he wants to be such an idiot, let him; in fact, I'll bring him upstairs, then I'll throw him out of my house.' I thought it would be fun to get my revenge. I was definitely into being a fifties cock tease and then leaving him with aching balls.

So I brought him upstairs by the elevator. He kissed me good night, then started getting more and more passionate. We were standing by the door, in the hallway, and he undid my dress at the back and then started touching me. I thought, 'Good! Maybe he'll actually do some decent foreplay for a while and then I can have an orgasm and throw him out! What the hell, I haven't had sex in a long time, I might as well take advantage of it.'

But as soon as I had just started to enjoy that, I looked down and suddenly he was unzipping his pants and pulling his dick out.

Then he just barely puts it in, he's just getting the tip in there, and I say, '*Stop right now!*' He immediately jumps back two feet and says, 'Why??!' (We're standing there, my dress is all undone, his pants are down on the floor around his ankles, etc.) I say, 'Look, Sam, I told you that it really bothered me when you didn't call me last time ... why did you go to all that trouble – dressing up, taking me out to dinner and driving me places. Why didn't you just stay home and jerk off?'

So that was how it ended, with him being ... stunned.

But wait a minute, aren't women supposed to be sexually 'in charge' now? Not 'victims' of men? Aren't those who can't handle all of this just 'neurotics' and 'non-achievers'?

The New Woman has got it together. And that means treating sex casually, behaving just 'like one of the guys'.

HAVING SEX FOR FUN

Of course women are not *always* on the defensive. Sometimes they like sex 'just for fun' too! While a lot of women say they usually prefer sex with feeling, most, at some point in their lives, also like to try playing around:

I love, love, *love* to explore men's bodies! They each have a different smell, a different touch.

I like to have sex with different men, to see how they will make love, what they do when they come. And whether they do it once, twice, or all night long!

When he walked in, I knew I was very attracted to him. He had dark curly hair, and he looked up at me from under his brows with brilliant blue eyes. We had a great dinner, got rather tipsy and he suggested we go back to my place. He said he was still hungry! We got to my flat and he sat in the living room while I rummaged around in the kitchen trying to make something to eat. All I had was stale rolls, but I thought, 'What the hell, he doesn't care, he'll eat them and think it's delicious.' So I'm standing there, swaying a bit from the wine, and trying to slice these rolls in half so they can fit in the toaster.

He came up behind me and kissed my neck. He smelled so good, and his body felt so strong and lithe against my back. I forgot the rolls, I forgot I was tired from a week's work, I forgot I was in my damned kitchen.

We went wild together and were on my kitchen floor in a matter of minutes. It was great. It was total abandon – my jewelry was in the sink, my clothes were strewn all over the place, my shoes were under the stove. He left at half past three, which pissed me off, but it was still great fun and some of the steamiest sex I have ever had.

One woman remembers in detail a fantastic night of sex with two male friends:

I was at home, and I was exhausted. I had been working hard and had just come home. I was not in the mood for fun.

I had just washed my face when the doorbell went. Keith and Brian, two friends of mine, were standing in the doorway in dinner suits. The conversation and course of events went something like this:

Me: Hi . . . What are you guys *doing*? (With a smile and a laugh of disbelief.)

Keith and Brian: We are here to please you. (Said in a sort of robot-like fashion.)

Me: What do you mean? I look like shit, I'm exhausted, I've just got home . . . I can't go out like *this*!

Keith and Brian: We are here to please you. Come with us, please.

They walk towards me with smiles on their faces. They pick me up off the floor and keep saying, 'Come with us, we are here to please you.' I start laughing uncontrollably. They carry me out to their car and put me in the front seat. They get in on either side, blindfold me, and wrap me in a warm blanket. They pour me a glass of very good champagne, and they take off.

They tell me jokes and give me more and more champagne. Soon, we pull over. Keith gets out of the car for about five minutes. I am still blindfolded.

He returns and we get out. They lead me forward and then unlock a door. Inside, they sit me down and I hear noises of clothing being taken off. They untie my blindfold. We are in a motel room. Keith and Brian stand before me in nothing but tight navy-blue underwear, and very wide smiles.

By this time I'm giggling helplessly, and feeling slightly tipsy and tired. They say the 'we are here to please you' line again, and I just say, 'Fine, do it.' I've given up trying to figure this out. What the hell.

Keith unzips a small suitcase as Brian leads me to the

bed and lies me down on my stomach. They turn out the lights. Brian sits at the head of the bed and Keith sits at the foot. They start to massage me through my clothes, strongly and deeply. It feels so good. They can tell that I am perfectly relaxed and enjoying this.

Soon, my shirt comes off. Then my bra. They are very intent on what they are doing, totally in tune with what feels good to me and what doesn't. It seems they really *are* there to please me!

After a while, Keith brings out a jar of honey, and they begin to apply it to my skin, very slowly and sensuously. Then they start to lick it off. With both of them working on me at the same time, I am slipping into oblivion. Nothing exists at the moment but this room and the three of us – nothing else matters. I am doing something illicit, something that I have never come close to doing before, and I am enjoying it.

Soon, we are all entwined with each other – I don't know who's kissing me or who I am kissing.

Finally Keith is inside me and Brian is lying next to me, touching me everywhere. Their hands and tongues and cocks are all over me. Then Brian is over me and puts his cock in my mouth, while Keith pushes himself inside me even harder. Brian moans and comes in my mouth and it tastes delicious. Then he moves Keith out of the way and licks me until I am about to explode, while Keith sucks my nipples. I am going absolutely *crazy* – it's really exciting, like my ultimate fantasy. I feel completely saturated with sex and delirious with pleasure. When it is over, we fall into an exhausted sleep.

The next morning they take me home. I look like I have not only been dragged through a hedge but have lived in the hedge for the evening and have been hit by a very large truck. My face is chapped from their beards. I'm still wondering if it really happened!

DO WOMEN WANT TO BE MONOGAMOUS?

What about when a woman goes out with one man, has sex with him, decides she doesn't like him or he never calls

45

again; goes out with a second man, has sex with him; then the first one calls back, they get together and so on? This leads inexorably, it seems, to multiple sexual partners. As one woman asked, 'How many men can you sleep with at the same time without being a "slut"?'

Most women want their boyfriends and lovers to be as monogamous, as they themselves are, inside a relationship:

> I think it's more important than ever to want monogamy. I always did, but now, with the disease of AIDS in the world, I can't imagine a relationship without it. But I can just imagine the quizzical looks I would get from men if, the first time I sleep with them, I would say, 'I think we should both get tested for AIDS, and then not sleep with anyone else.' They would act like, 'What gives her the right to make demands like that?' I always wanted to make demands like that, really. It's weird that now I have the possibility of disease on my side.

Another woman wrote to her lover about how she feels about his affair:

> I can't live with the knowledge that you are thinking of and possibly actually fucking others behind my back. That you would/could try and brainwash me into believing that it was just a one-time thing, then Hope comes up, then Robin comes up – God knows who else was with you – is incredible to me. That you could lie to me is incredible. But what's really incredible is that you should *want* that. I have found myself craving sexual and emotional attention from men ... lately, but I know that I only feel it because I don't have it from you. I want it so much from you – but you are not there for me (really, or consistently), so I look for it in others, at least the possibility of it anyway. But for you? Why you need others is something I find hard to comprehend. The line about your French blood (that French men need mistresses) is the stupidest

thing I have ever heard, so I'm not even going to go into that.

But other women see it quite differently:

My friends cannot understand how I can be happy to love a man who sleeps with other women. I sleep with other men, too. They think it's 'weird', and that we 'just *think* we're happy'. But we really are! I feel guilty sometimes for not agonizing over this the way they would want me to!'

Even with the advent of AIDS, I still am not ready to have a monogamous relationship. I just don't want one. I want to be free to have sex with whoever I choose.

It's funny, but it's harder than you think to find men who want this, too. They want to be able to screw around, but they don't want you to be able to! I do insist that they tell me if they sleep with someone, and that they are sure about that person's sexual history, and I tell them the same.

FLIRTING AND POWER

Many women enjoy flirting and 'teasing' men, seeing it as a lot of fun, just for its own sake – without necessarily leading to intercourse:

To be honest, I really enjoy male attention, dressing up and being sexy. I don't like a lot of their attitudes, but I like attracting them.

I have to admit, I think it's fun to look and act a way I know will drive a man I am trying to provoke *crazy*! I *want* him to see me and get a big hard-on – and later tell me how he could hardly control himself out in the restaurant or whatever.

I know that women are supposed to feel degraded when they are considered as sex objects, and I have. But I also like to be wanted a lot by a lot of men, at a bar or on the street. It's a rush.

The fun part here, according to most women, is 'getting him to want you'. Although women are aware of the injustice of being seen as no more than a sexual commodity, some feel there is a flip-side to this: through the age-old game of flirtation, they can turn the tables on men. Here they have the power, however temporary, to be in control of the man for a change.

As opposed to most men's idea of 'getting laid' as the final goal, sometimes all women really want is to know that they are desired:

> I love to turn them on and have them almost desperate to touch me. It's a great feeling.

> I *always* felt the most power and security when I knew a man wanted me. The feeling of being wanted was a great 'high' for me. Like when they told me I was sexy and said so with awe in their voices. I liked it. I felt like I was in charge of whether I 'gave' or 'withheld', that I ran the show.

> I was and am considered 'sexy', whatever that means. I think it's when I discovered that sexiness is where a woman's power lies.

Another woman recounts how she denied her drive to be flirtatious.

> When the women's movement began I jumped into it whole-heartedly, became 'political' and stopped wearing make-up and tight clothes. Men had always told me how sexy I was but I said, 'So what? God gave me this, I didn't do anything to get it. What about my mind? My politics? My brain?' I meant that. But when they stopped telling me I was gorgeous, I hated it! I realized that although I had always wanted to be taken seriously, I also enjoyed being wanted and desired sexually. It's a strong feeling, one of power, and I missed that particular kind of power. I like to be lusted after.

If men didn't insist on seeing us as *either* sexy (and stupid) *or* intelligent, and if men didn't see 'sexual women' as less morally 'right', we wouldn't have to make this choice. *They* don't.

Is dressing sexy anti-feminist?

Other women argue that dressing in a sexy style or flirting is 'selling out' and buying into the submissive behavior we have used to get the favors of men, since they have more power and money than we do.

Some women feel angry and frustrated with the pressure to 'dress for success' with men – to model their physical appearance on stereotyped male taste:

> With my big crush, I tried all the tricks. I tried innocent, I tried dirty. I tried athletic, I tried country, I tried downright obscene. Sometimes I 'passed', sometimes I didn't.

> I used to dress outrageously as a kind of statement – to show I didn't need anyone's approval. This was not true – just the opposite! But I *did* get approval this way (sort of) because some men would be attracted by this 'challenge'. I later realized this wasn't very satisfying. What the hell was wrong with just plain me?

> When I met him, it was clear I did not 'fit' into his social circle. I didn't dress or act like you are supposed to, to be a woman appropriate to his group. But I realized almost immediately that I could only really have him if I conformed to his true requirements and expectations. Well, I didn't even have to guess, he actually *told* me what I should wear and look like.
> Inside, I was outraged, but I knew that if I wanted him, I would have to do it. I hid my rage, dressed in friends' clothes, and actually dyed my hair blond! He loved it. But I felt awful. I couldn't carry on this charade for more than a few months. It was too exhausting! I didn't want him enough for that.

If we as women are constantly being told that we have to 'catch a man', and if make-up and sexual adornment are one of the ways to do that, then they can be considered symbols of our lack of self-worth and pride. Indeed, the amount of money we spend on cosmetics, and the amount of time we spend worrying about our weight (as compared to men, who don't seem to care as much), does indicate that we are very concerned about being attractive.

On the other hand, our interest in beauty and fabrics, clothes and home decoration are perhaps things we should be praised for, and interests men too should develop. These have often been women's greatest means of self-expression, or of making a statement, when interesting jobs and creative professions were closed to us. Women *and* men have used adornment since at least the beginning of classical civilization. Severity in women's appearance does not automatically provide anyone with power, and to insist that 'serious' women (or men) dress rigidly is no magic route to equally shared power.

Each woman has the right to choose her own way to work for the empowerment of women, and this includes the right to make her own choices about dress and the style of her relationships with men.

DATE RAPE

The pressure to have sex is at its worst when it reaches the stage where 'giving in to keep him happy' amounts to a form of rape, a violation of your desires and body – 'date rape':

I definitely didn't want to sleep with him the first night, it was just too soon. It never occurred to me that he would put up a fight about it. I thought he liked me. He started to hold me down with one arm and unzip his fly at the same time. I laughed at first when he held me down, I thought he was just playing. But then I saw that what *I* wanted was of no importance to him – in fact he wasn't even thinking about it. I said no, again and again, but it was clear he wasn't going to stop, and he was big. I was scared to kick him or put up a fight, and I was confused. This was a nice guy that I really liked. I let him do it. Yes, I was aroused, but I still felt dirty. It was horrible, and I knew I could never trust him again.

I really liked this man, so I agreed to have dinner with him. We had a good time, but when the bill came, he offered me 'dessert at his place'. I went because I couldn't imagine that he would try the old 'let's see how fast I can get her into bed' routine – he seemed such a gentleman. When we got there he dimmed the lights and put some jazz on the stereo and got me some ice-cream. Then he sat next to me. Then he lay next to me. All the time I'm thinking, 'Oh, I'm so disappointed this is happening,' but I knew that if I said something he would tell me I had hang-ups and it would turn into a big scene. So I lay there and tried to continue talking, but it was clear he had only one thing on his mind. I gave up and let him get on with it. I didn't enjoy it at all, but it was far less uncomfortable than going through the whole conversation about why I didn't want to.

Another woman recalls a vivid, recent experience of date rape:

I was with a group of people, many of whom I did not know. I was depressed over the failure of a relationship, and had just stopped by to say hello and was going to go home early. Then I noticed a very attractive blond man who kept looking at me and smiling. I thought he had a nice smile, but I wasn't that interested. It took too much effort.

I walked over to get a cup of coffee, and he was there, immediately. He was very talkative, introduced himself and chatted with me. He seemed bright and interesting. It was really nice to feel someone found me attractive and interesting when I had just had such a blow to my heart and ego.

51

We went out to the corner for a cup of coffee and talked for a while. He told me he had just divorced, had a little daughter whom he loved, was a fashion photographer. We found that we knew some people in common. I was getting more and more interested, energized by his attention. He asked me back to his flat. To this day, I can't believe I went.

I don't know what I was thinking, I had only just met him. I would never normally do that. I guess I was in a what-the-hell mood and was feeling so sad that my judgement was off. Very off.

We got to his flat and went inside. It was comfortable and pleasant. He showed me photographs and they were really quite good. He had a very child-like quality, very appealing. He got excited over whatever we were talking about. Now I *really* thought he was good-looking.

He suggested we watch Star Trek IV, which I thought was just about the most boring thing I could imagine. I mean, here I was, with this trendy, hip fashion photographer and he wanted to watch Star Trek IV!

He pulled my chair next to his and kissed me a little. It was nice. He touched me and that was nice, too. As he started to lift up my dress, I said I had to go soon. He said, 'No, you don't,' and kept going. I stood up, but he pulled me back down really violently and said, 'God, are you hung up or something? I mean, we met, we like each other, what's the matter? Don't you allow yourself to have any fun? What's the matter with you?' He was shouting and his face scared me.

I couldn't believe it. I mean, I had heard about these kinds of things happening to other women, but I never thought it would happen to me.

I told him it was nothing to do with having fun. I said that I would feel lousy about it in the morning, and didn't he know it was 1988 and there was a disease called AIDS that was killing everybody, and how could we have sex so casually with that knowledge? He sort of rolled his eyes and said, 'Oh, God, that' (pointing to his crotch) 'is clean. Don't worry, I mean, I have a healthy daughter, I've been married for five years.'

I was going to say that had nothing to do with it because it didn't tell me who his wife had slept with while they were married and who he had slept with since his 'monogamy' had expired. It just wasn't worth it.

He gave me such a hard time that I ended up jerking him off just so he would leave me alone and let me out of the flat (he had locked the door).

The next day I felt very depressed and bad about myself, and very dirty. He called me incessantly for about two weeks. I never returned the calls.

Many types of advice have been given about how to deal with a potential rape situation. If you think you are in danger, the obvious thing to do is to move – *fast*! Out of the room or front door, or wherever you are. Or get to a telephone and call for help. If there are other people in the building or nearby, scream very loudly.

One way to really turn someone off, although it may be difficult in a terrifying situation, is to act your way out of it. Assume as ugly and unappealing a demeanor as possible: twitch, drool, contort yourself. If he thinks you're about to have a seizure of some sort, he may well be scared off and he certainly won't see you as a sexual object.

If you think he is dangerous or he is threatening physical violence, one way to diffuse the situation, if there is no way out, may be to jerk him off just to play for time. After he has come he will be much less interested in rape. His mood will have changed, and you will gain a valuable few minutes while he recovers to get out of there. Of course, jerking him off will also avoid possible AIDS contamination – no matter how unpleasant it may be.

Date rape is an extremely serious issue, with an increasing number of women reporting such occurrences. The current climate of upholding 'family values' is doing nothing to encourage men to think about what they are doing, nor question why they still try to 'seduce' and pressure women into sex. The pressure, as usual, is on women to modify *their* behavior: to learn again to 'say no'. While that is never a bad skill, why is it still assumed that men's behavior is 'normal', and ours is put down to 'psychology'?

AIDS: HAS IT STOPPED ANY OF THE MEN YOU KNOW?

The AIDS epidemic may make us all look very closely at our sexual behavior and think twice about leaping into bed with someone we know very little about. However, many women are finding that men rarely volunteer information about their sexual history. It seems they can be just as inconsiderate about AIDS protection as they have been in the past about birth control (when the 'only' risk was pregnancy). With birth control, men often assume that a woman is on the Pill or that she's using another method of contraception ('It's none of my business as long as whatever it is doesn't get in the way'). However, for protection from AIDS, the decision has to be mutual and can't be hidden.

Using a condom during coitus is the best way for both partners to avoid AIDS. There is a small possibility (statistically less than for coitus) of contracting AIDS if you don't use a condom during oral sex, especially fellatio. Although fellatio to orgasm is the most likely to be unsafe, even fellatio for stimulation only can produce pre-ejaculatory fluid: the drop of fluid that appears on the tip of the penis long before ejaculation. Ingestion of this could be unsafe. Also, a man might contract the virus during cunnilingus.

Despite the spread of AIDS, however, few men take time in the early stages of a passionate embrace to say that they have a condom and plan to use it. One woman asked her lover why he didn't raise the subject when they first slept together. 'I assumed you were protected,' he replied, 'and that you would have told me if you had AIDS.'

More and more women find that in order to protect themselves, it's necessary to take the initiative. But many women feel that this puts them in an impossible position: if she comes prepared, he may think she's an 'easy lay', but if she doesn't, she can't depend on him to be responsible. So, as one woman puts it:

I'd almost rather not have sex than have to deal with it – I mean, bring it up, feel weird, not trust each other.

THE CONDOM CONVERSATION

So how do you bring up birth control or AIDS prevention the first time you have sex?

The straightforward approach

The direct approach is by far the easiest if you are with a man who is sensible and aware. If he doesn't offer one, at least you can expect that he will not be shocked, pissed off or insulted by your request. When things are getting heated, just reach over to your little box on the bedside table and pull out a condom, turn and smile at him. He will probably smile too and take it from you.

The assuming approach

Sometimes it is hard to know how a man is going to react, so one way to bring up condoms is by acting as if you *assume* that he is going to use one. 'The condoms are in that box,' or, 'Make sure the condom doesn't fall out of your pocket,' shows that you expect that he has one and is going to use it, or that he was just about to ask you where you keep yours. Also, 'Can you believe that some men actually expect a woman to have casual sex without a condom *today*?' shows that you assume he is not quite so stupid. This may shame him into behaving more responsibly than he had intended, or massage his ego so that he will never tell you that he hadn't even thought about condoms until you brought them up! Either way, the result is that he will use one, which is what matters.

The brainy approach

'Did you hear the statistics on how many people will contract AIDS in the heterosexual community in the next five years?' This may dampen his passion momentarily, but it should also interrupt his lust long enough to make him think about what he is doing. You don't want to engage him in a long conversation – 'I saw an interesting program last night about how the HIV virus is transmitted,' or, 'Have you bought shares in a Rubber Company?' – but you *do* want to let him know that you are responsible, know about 'safe' sex and care about your health.

The funny approach

'Ever seen the rainbow-striped, ribbed sort before?' or, 'Would you like a cocktail and a condom, or just a condom?' are a couple of suggestions. Anything to break the tension of what can be a difficult moment will work. Sometimes playing hide-the-condom is fun (in pillows, in your under-wear, between the pages of a magazine). Hopefully, your new lover has a sense of humor and is willing to make using a condom fun instead of a passion-killer.

The sexy approach

As you and your lover are heading towards the bed, in the last stages of undress, imagining total nudity and abandon, turn to him, and in a low, sexy voice say: 'I want you inside me. I want all of you. I want to put this on you.' Most men will find this hard to resist. Your lover will be all the more impassioned as you push him down, straddle him, tear the condom packet open with your teeth, and slowly slide it on him. Keep talking in a low, husky voice all the while. It can be great fun!

The tempting approach

Even though we know no one should get a medal for wearing a condom when you ask them to, it can sometimes be helpful to show a man how much you appreciate his co-operation. If he is a nice guy but hasn't dealt with this moment before, this will make it more comfortable for both of you. 'I have some delicious ways to kiss your body that I would love to show you, but you have to wear this first,' or, 'You can't know the surprises I have in store for you as soon as you put this on,' are sexy and enticing, and will make him feel using a condom will definitely be worth it.

The reassuring approach

Some men fear that they won't 'feel you' as much with a condom, that they may lose their erection or not be the 'perfect lover' if they take time to put one on. If it affects his erection slightly, it helps to let him know that this is OK, that you are not disappointed; kiss him until the fear and discomfort of the moment passes.

'Get out of my bedroom, you ape!'

Unfortunately, there are still men out there who think that condoms are out of date and an insult to their manhood. Anything over *their* cock is tantamount to castration! Hopefully, a man like this will never see your bedroom. But first impressions can be misleading and we all make mistakes. So if you find yourself in a passionate embrace with a man who is still refusing to wear a condom, there is only one answer. Don't have sex with him – show him the door!

WHAT IF AIDS IS A REALITY FOR YOU?

Increasing numbers of women are being infected by the HIV virus. If you are HIV positive, how will you tell potential sexual partners? Will you find it just too difficult? Not only is there the personal anguish to deal with, but social/sexual situations become even more difficult, as this young woman describes:

> I am HIV positive. I haven't had sex in a year and a half. You cannot imagine how difficult sex has become for me. And in a way I'm not even interested in having

it. It's not only that I worry how they would react if I told them, but I also worry because I could pass it on. Telling them is only half of it.

I went to some counseling centers, but they were all gay males there. At first when I found out I tested positive, I panicked. I haven't told my parents. I feel alone a lot because I can't talk to anyone. I have a counselor, she tells me to drink orange juice! She doesn't know how I really feel – in the morning I shake and have huge bouts of depression. To go out, I have to put on a completely different face to how I feel.

When I told some friends of mine they became really abusive . . . they assumed I had had lots of sex, that that's why I got it!

Someone said that 'loneliness is everyone's great fear'. I feel really lonely sometimes. My father wants me to get married, he doesn't know. Think of it – falling passionately in love and just knowing it can never be! So meanwhile, if I'm kissing someone, I just break away.

I never thought I would get AIDS, but I did. I want to kill the bloody bastard who did it. He didn't tell me. A one-night stand. He was a rugby player – it was something that just happened one night. I confronted him with it later. He was really surprised I knew.

I go out and forget who I really am. I'm really mad. It's like schizophrenia, living this way. I found out I had it when I got pneumonia. At the hospital they said, 'She's only twenty and she's got pneumonia?' That's when they decided to check me out for AIDS.

Now I'm really turned off to the idea of penetration. But I'm not attracted to women either. I find the idea of sex repulsive. I'm twenty-one, I'm young, and I'm scared of dying. I don't have time to worry about sex. I find I like being alone in an odd way. I go home and write things down. I want to be alone, and I long to be with others. I don't know, it's just an impossible thing.

UNDEFINING SEXUALITY

So where do we stand in this brave new world of sexuality? Are things better for women? AIDS and some birth control methods have increased potential health risks, but the double standard is not as strong as it was, even though many men (and some women) still subscribe to the virgin-whore school of thought.

The area of least change has been in the definition of sex itself. Since the publication of the first *Hite Report* in 1976, there is no longer the same pressure on women to have orgasm only from 'penetration', to fake orgasm during coitus or to be 'ashamed' of clitoral stimulation. Awkwardness and other problems may remain in these areas, but the question of what 'sexuality' is has hardly begun to be explored.

Women often love sensuality, 'foreplay', flirting, dressing up and being looked at, looking at the other person, kissing and making out, without 'going all the way'. Why don't men like these things as much? Or, if they do, why do they feel they must rush on quickly to have intercourse? Is it because, once aroused, they are frightened of losing their erection ('better to "put it in" while I have it than take a chance of losing it')?

Having sex on his terms

One of the worst pressures women feel is the pressure to disregard their own needs, whether physical, emotional or psychological, to please men in bed:

I often feel pressured into sex by my lover. Also pressured into liking sex – being told that what feels good to him ought to be my primary satisfaction. I pressure myself. I often try to make my vagina please me, but without real confidence that it can. I do it to end the tension of his wanting sex, to maintain the relationship despite my doubts, to justify my anger against him. The pressure to be open to whatever feels good to the man is sometimes overwhelming.

59

I like this man so much and want him to like me as much that I'll do almost anything. It makes me very embarrassed to say this. But I will. If he wants me to dress up in weird clothes or talk to him about other women and things when we are having sex, I do it. I wish I was enough.

I learned very early on that pleasing a man in bed was a primary source of power, if not my only one. I learned as much as I could, acting the way I found men liked, learning from them what they wanted me to do, be, say. It was a worthwhile pursuit: this was a very powerful skill to have. But I was having sex and pleasing men for four years before I even knew what it felt like to have an orgasm with a man.

I hate getting up from bed, sweaty and exhausted, having nearly killed myself with acting as though I was in ecstasy, having to go into the bathroom and 1) clean up, and 2) make myself come before going to sleep. I wonder if other women feel like this.

I have to act as though it's OK with me if he just decides to get up and leave because there's a good game on TV and he wants to watch it with his friends! That is *not* OK with me. It's not very romantic.

My lover is very sensitive, but I think it would really upset him to know I don't get as turned on as he thinks I do when we make love. I want to tell him, but it's too late now. Now our sex life is set. I was just so scared that he would leave and find someone else that I faked it every time. Now I can't stop, or maybe he might leave. I couldn't bear that.

Are women and men sexually at odds?

Women often value different sexual activities to men. For example, most women enjoy clitoral stimulation at least as much as intercourse. Men orgasm easily from intercourse, while most women orgasm most easily from exterior clitoral stimulation. Women also tend to like longer periods of sensuality, embracing, feeling and touching. On the other hand, both women and men seem to love touching head-to-toe in a complete body embrace. Strangely, our language does not even have a word for this.

One woman describes her current struggle to express her sexuality with her boyfriend – who is not helping:

My anger with him began very quickly with the first intercourse. First, I was resistant to sex at that moment, and felt that he ignored this in his typically male intense desire to complete the act, as if that would couple us even without my co-operation. I feel that fucking is much more pleasurable for him than for me, that the whole system is geared toward the pretense that fucking is the epitome of sexuality.

I've told him that I don't usually orgasm from intercourse and that when I do, it's less intense and satisfying than a clitoral orgasm. I've been telling him this for almost two years. He keeps trying to think of it as a temporary condition – because otherwise, he says, it ruins something for him. He always dreamed of finding a woman who would respond to him, to his penis. He says this is something that takes away the whole pornographic, sadistic image of the man as taking, and makes him a giver.

What I keep trying to tell him is that it wouldn't matter to me – that I'd be more than happy to give in that way – if he would accept *my* sexuality as it is. I've never felt accepted by him for what feels best to me; we are always at cross-purposes and trying to accomplish the impossible.

I feel guilty for not coming from fucking. I'm afraid he's going to leave me for someone who'll pretend to come from fucking, who'll lie, or who doesn't know any better. He feels guilty for wanting the turn-on of a woman who really loves fucking. The funny thing is that what turns me on most about fucking is how good it feels to him.

I'd like to ask women how they live with men, how they enjoy sex, until I get some real answers. I've talked about not coming from intercourse with two or three women – it makes me mad that men can have such reliable pleasure from sex and we can't. Usually from women I get the feeling that it's just one of those things they've learned to live with.

How Real Men have sex

Do we really know what male sexuality is? While the pressure is definitely on women to adapt to men's sexual needs, we may not really know what men's 'needs' are. The definition of male sexuality as a driving desire for 'penetration' is quite clearly culturally exaggerated;* male sexuality comprises a much larger, more varied group of physical feelings than erection, penetration and ejaculation.

However, men are still being socially pressured to express their sexuality in this one way. Not only is there enormous pressure on women to provide sexual services for men, but also men are expected to continually pressure women for sex as traditionally defined: penetration. The definition of sex as 'foreplay' followed by 'vaginal penetration' (why not call it 'penile covering'?) and ending with male orgasm should definitely be 'undefined'.

There are many, many other ways to express and enjoy sexuality, some genital and some not. Historically, coitus was not always the basic definition of sex. In classical Greece men had sex with other men so much as a matter of course that they had to be reminded to have sex with their wives 'at least three times a month' – for fear that they would not reproduce. But even here we see an emphasis on genitalia that might not always be present in a more sensual definition or expression of sexuality.

* The theory that 'sex' as we know it is part of an ideology, a cultural and not a biological definition, was first put forth in *The Hite Report on Female Sexuality*, published in 1976 (reissued in Pandora, 1989), not by Michel Foucault in 1981, as is often stated.

TOWARDS A MORE EROTIC SEXUALITY

More and more women (and some men) are now questioning whether coitus is 'naturally' and always *the* basic
definition of sex. For example, is it sex when no penetration
takes place? Of course it is. Intercourse (penetration)
became the primary focus of sex, glorified in patriarchal
religions, because a high rate of reproduction was desired,
and because it was considered crucial that lineage go
through men (hence the ownership or control of women
and their sexuality).

But why can't sex be seen as an individual vocabulary
of gestures and feelings – different for each person,
and different in each relationship? How do *you* really
feel?

It will help both you and your partner or partners if you
can sort out exactly what your needs are, where they might
be in conflict, and where there are ways to experiment with
new forms of intimacy. If both women and men could be
completely honest about their sexuality, it would help to
avoid the pressures to feel 'sexual' on someone else's terms,
to be a 'sexy' person, and to have sex even when you don't
really feel like it.

So, stop, wait, think during sex: is this really what you
want to be doing? Or is there some other kind of physical
expression you might prefer?

A good way to think honestly about what sex means to
you is to ask yourself the following probing questions.
Then try asking your lover the second set of questions.

Questions to ask yourself

• What is sex with your partner usually like? Do you
enjoy it? Do you usually come? When?

• Which is the easiest way for you to come: masturbation,
clitoral stimulation, oral sex, intercourse? Do you like your
legs open or closed? Does your lover know this?

• If you don't come from intercourse, have you told a
woman friend about this? How did it feel to tell her?

- Have you told your lover that you don't come from intercourse? How did he react? Did you tell him that most women don't? How did that make you feel?

- Have you ever masturbated with a lover? How did it feel to do that? Was it a turn on? If you haven't done this, would you like to?

- When do you feel the most passionate? How do you show this? Do you become more aggressive? Or do you want to be 'taken'? Do you like playing different roles?

- Do you use fantasies to help you come? Which ones?

- Do you masturbate when your lover is not around? Do you think about him, or other fantasies? Do you tell him this?

- What do you think of pornography? Do you like it? If so, do you prefer literature, photos or films? Do you like to watch/read them with your lover? Does he look at it alone? How does that make you feel?

- Do you feel turned on in emotionally intense moments or do you prefer sex in quiet, cozy, safe moments?

- Would you rather have sex or an expensive dinner out?

- How do you feel about going down on your lover? Do you feel in control? Does it turn you on? Or do you feel used?

- Do you prefer manual stimulation of your clitoris, or oral? Do you feel uncomfortable asking your lover for oral sex?

- Do you like to hear 'I love you' during sex? Do you like to say it?

Questions to ask your lover

- Where do you *really* feel your orgasm? At the top of your penis? At the base? Inside your body? Where?

- Would you still like sex if you couldn't have head-to-toe body contact during it? Would you like sex without kissing?

• How often do you have sex just because you want to come? Do you think it is more manly to have intercourse than to masturbate?

• Do you enjoy sex without vaginal penetration?

• How do you feel if I go into the bathroom and wash after you come inside me? Do you think I'm being fastidious, or do you think I think you're dirty? Do you prefer it if I don't wash afterwards?

• Would you rather I went down on you or had intercourse? Why?

• Do you worry that you might have AIDS? Do you worry that I might have AIDS? Do you think that we should both have a test?

• Do you ever masturbate when I'm not around? If you do, how often do you do it? What do you think about?

• Do you think my period is an exciting event? What are your biggest fears about it? Do you mind getting my blood on you or the bed? Do you want to avoid oral sex during it?

• Do you feel that it is normal for a woman to come from intercourse alone? Do you feel bad if I don't? Resentful? Guilty? Do you wonder what to do next?

• Do you feel confident giving me an orgasm with your hand on my clitoris? Do you ever feel impatient when I'm getting physical stimulation and you're not? What do you think about?

• How do you feel if I make myself come? Are you turned on? Bored? Upset? Or have you never noticed?

• How do you feel about the fact that many women need to have their legs together to come? Would you like to know more about women's anatomy?

Eroticism is a vast, largely unexplored area which includes dressing up, playing, talking, making up stories, posing, inviting someone else to be involved sensually with you. Passion and desire are part of it – the desire not only to have orgasm, but to lie together, to press bodies together, tightly, as tightly as possible; to lie feeling the other breathe as they sleep, their breath grazing your cheek and mingling with your own; to smell their body, caress their mouth with your mouth, know the smell and taste of their genitals, to feel your finger inside them, to caress the opening of their buttocks, to lose yourself in all the feelings there are.

—3—

Fighting: A Radical New Analysis

We have so many horrible scenes. They all happen at his place or at mine, or on the phone in the middle of the night. I often wish I had a tape recorder to record the things he says and what goes on, because later he denies most of what he's said, but *I* always remember him behaving really mean.

He stalked out of the house breaking pottery he had made. He was totally 'out of control' and I let him rage awhile and then held him and told him how glad I was he finally 'let go'. His biggest fear was that I really didn't like him. He always said that first when we fought through these conflicts. I was really overwhelmed, sad and angry, but on some level I knew he had to get a lot of stuff out.

BEHIND CLOSED DOORS

Fighting belongs to a private world – something painful that can happen between two people when they are alone. No one else is there, so no one else knows exactly what goes on. In these moments, it is difficult to perceive the dynamics of the situation clearly, see how to stop what is going on, or get a just hearing for one's feelings.

In this chapter we will strip away the isolation, end the 'unseen' nature of what goes on. We will lay bare the patterns as women describe them. Renaming them realis-

67

tically is a first step in changing them, so that women will have a different way of fighting, of reacting to negative situations in their relationships in the 1990s.

'Are fights this bad for others?'

Women talk to each other about fights they have had, but even if their friends are sympathetic and say they know what it's like, many women still won't tell even their best friends the worst parts of what goes on, for fear of being thought less of. They wonder if anyone else's fights are really as bad as theirs.

Fights feel like a private jungle where there are no rules, no outside observers, and no clear 'truce' or 'victory' – and they often leave women feeling very isolated and alone:

When I fight with him I feel so alone. I usually wind up feeling fairly destroyed too. It starts when he hurts my feelings. I tell him, and hope he will apologize, take it back, say he didn't mean it. But he gets mad and says I'm causing trouble, I'm nagging him and he won't have it. Then I get more upset, and scream at him or cry. He just gets silent, and refuses to talk at all. I feel I am horrible, and should be ashamed for screaming – and I feel ashamed of what he did to me, too. Plus, I think I look neurotic. Finally, I usually want so much for it to be over that I end up apologizing. I feel terrible.

It was six months since we had had our first date, and I wanted to do something special, so I went out and got white balloons and streamers and put them up all over my bedroom and bed. Then I bought a sexy lingerie outfit in white lace with garters and everything. He walked in and was totally non-plussed, said something about it looking nice, nothing about *me* looking nice, and said he was really tired from working and he was just going to go home and go to sleep. He didn't stop to think I would be upset by that. I lay there and cried in the dark so hard I thought my eyes were going to pop out of my face. At six in the morning, I got up and tore all the balloons and streamers down. I couldn't wait to throw them away; I felt so angry with myself for putting them up at all. When I saw him later that day, he asked me why I was so upset. I just looked at him. What could I say?

We go round and round in our fights. The other day I said I didn't want to get together, I wanted to stay at home and read the paper and watch TV by myself. He was furious. Then the whole thing started as usual: 'Why can't you see me tonight and do that another night? You really are so selfish.' In the end I gave in and let him come over and watch some stupid thing on TV that I hated. Our fights are never resolved, he always gets his way, and I end up crying in the bathroom in the middle of the night while he gets his beauty sleep after a good screw.

Women often feel they should be 'together' enough to stop fighting like this, so they hide it like a secret shame. In fact the most common way of 'dealing' with the problem is to try to hide it from outsiders, so that nobody will know. Women feel they can't tell people because it is usually not the 'bully' who is blamed, but the 'bullied'. (She must somehow be 'weak' and 'deserves it', or else why did she pick him?)

BRINGING UP THE ISSUES

Why most fights start

Sometimes small disagreements or hurt feelings can turn into something major because of an underlying fear on the part of one or both people that the other doesn't really love them, 'hates' them, is going to reject them. But with goodwill this can be resolved, as mutual assurances are given.

However, there are other types of fights. While we can all be beastly at times, it is extremely common for fights to begin with the small acts of emotional aggression, or emotional bullying, women described in Chapter 1. After a woman has noticed a series of such incidents, or feels vaguely uncomfortable but is not really sure why, she may try to 'bring up' the problem, or describe how she is feeling.

This often leads to the next stage of a potential fight: the man denying there is a problem or refusing to discuss the issue, whether through stony silence or a series of condescending put-downs.

For example, if a woman 'complains' (tries to bring up a problem for discussion), she may be asked, 'Why are you making waves? I feel fine!', or told, 'Now, don't start being a nagging, complaining woman. I thought you were different,' or, 'I don't know what's wrong with you, I didn't *do* anything.'

When I am upset because of one of his condescending remarks, and say so, it's always, 'It's just a *word*, babe.' Or if today's problem is that I cooked a lovely meal for him and he didn't say anything about it, it's, 'Hey, it was good, I ate it, OK?' I can't make him see that these things are not little things to me. The things I think are the most important he thinks are the least important.

When I want to talk about something that's bothering me in the relationship, he looks beleaguered, starts rolling his eyes: 'Oh, poor me, I'm so badgered by this complaining bitch.' He tells me I 'jump all over' him for 'no reason'! But I'm telling him there *is* a reason, *I* am upset! He just refuses to talk about it.

It is hardly surprising that women in relationships like these feel angry and hurt, unsettled, when the men who supposedly love them ignore their attempts to talk things over – even refuse to listen!

This then leads to a further escalation of the situation. The woman is now experiencing a double hurt or injustice. Probably at this point she is upset and is beginning to show it.

What happens then? Many men, unfortunately, bought into the social convention that women are 'overly emotional' (men 'know better'). When they see a woman 'upset', they are apt to put her down, tell her she is 'over-reacting', not listen to what she is really saying, nor consider her point of view to be as valid as their own. They do not seem to realize the self-serving, convenient nature of the stereotypes they are accepting and using.

Being put down for raising the issue

Although there are women who say that communication is good in their relationships, most describe being hurt and upset when they meet a brick wall of indifference or an aggressive refusal to talk during these 'discussions' with the man in their relationship:

> When I try to bring something up, he says, 'Don't even *start*.' He says those words to me before I've even begun.

> I can't seem to feel safe to say anything that's bothering me. He either tells me I don't make sense, that I'm crazy, or that he 'really can't take this anymore' (as though he will leave if I 'keep it up'). I feel it wouldn't happen if he would just listen. Then it could be resolved between us and we would be closer, and happy. The way it is, it just snowballs until I am either crying my eyes out at home or, worse, in front of him, and then I get totally quiet and submissive, just to keep the peace.

One woman tells an amazing story of how the man she loved blocked communication in a particularly hurtful way:

> I was telling him that I was pregnant. It was very hard for me to make the words come out of my mouth, I was so nervous and scared and felt so sick. All he did was look at me, and say, 'How do I know it's mine?' I couldn't believe it. It was the last thing I expected, or needed to hear.

The man's indifference to this woman's feelings is a form of emotional violence. It is also typical in that it shows how

71

some men change the subject or 'miss the point' in a way that wounds the other person. As we saw in Chapter 1, there are many forms of emotional violence, but they all involve aggressive or indifferent acts of one form or another.

However, we can laugh about some of these situations – they can be pretty funny, when you think about them later. Let's look at the most common reactions women say they encounter in fights. It's impossible not to laugh.

SEVEN CRAZED REACTIONS MEN HAVE WHEN WOMEN BRING UP PROBLEMS

'I feel fine. Why are you complaining?'

Many women find men can be maddeningly unresponsive to any hint of a grievance or complaint. As one said,

> His attitude when I am upset is usually, 'I feel fine. Why are you complaining?' Or, if I keep on, and get really upset, he will say, 'You're causing scenes.' Or he'll say, 'Why do you have to insist on making your point?' to which I say, 'I'm not "insisting" – I'm trying to talk to you!'

In other words, the man in this scenario is saying he doesn't care or want to know about what the woman is saying. Even without bothering to listen to her, he believes that she is wrong:

> It's always me that has 'all the problems', it's never him. He says I always want to 'drag things up'. It never occurs to him that my being upset has something to do with what he did! He thinks it's all my own weird hang-ups.

Implicit in this attitude is the idea that the woman is always finding something 'wrong' with the man, or *trying* to find things to criticize, and that if she wouldn't keep 'creating' problems, everything would be fine:

His opinion is that I'm criticizing him whenever I try to bring up anything that's bothering me, or that he has done to hurt me. He tells me I am just making trouble. He doesn't really listen to what I am saying. Usually I try to talk to him calmly first, and get no response, so then I yell and he tells me I am attacking him. I can't win.

The silent treatment

Men often try to shut women up with the classic silent treatment. The result is that the woman either shouts and a fight ensues, or she too becomes silent and cold. Either way, the 'problem' may never be resolved:

Until he 'resigns himself' to a talk, I meet with resistance all the way . . . I am talking and talking and getting little um-hmms.

What usually happens is I get upset about something and try to tell him. He says nothing. I get worked up trying to get a response, and then he finally says, 'What do you want from me?' which upsets me even more because he's not saying how he feels or even reacting to what I'm talking about!

He could just as well be a stuffed dummy for all the communication I get with him. He just looks at me and says nothing. Absolutely nothing. And, after I've worked myself up into a tantrum trying to get a response, if I stop for ten seconds (having asked him a question for the fiftieth time), he says, 'Have you finished?'

I do the talking, he just sits there and grunts. Then I yell, and he grunts some more.

He has a classic pose. He sits immobile, looking 'above it all' – the Mussolini pose, I call it. Aloof, while I try to get through to him.

Male nagging is silent. Silent sulking, or silent, arrogant disapproval.

73

I usually decide just to swallow my anger and resentment towards him because when I bring them up he gets so furious and it always ends up being really, really bad.

Pretending it never happened

Women also talk about how they feel when the man in their relationship 'deals' with something they bring up by simply ignoring the fact that they have said anything:

> I was very angry the other night before a couple were coming over for dinner. I was amazed at his ability to just slide right on through the evening as though nothing had happened. I am always amazed by that. Either he should join the Royal Shakespeare Company or he is the coldest and most two-faced person I have ever met. When they left, he was all cuddly and sweet and wanted to make wild passionate love. I felt *totally* depressed.

> We were on the phone. I was telling him that I needed some time alone with him. I thought he would welcome this talk and be eager to help (wishful thinking). He just glossed over the whole thing as though I had never said it, and went on to mention a party we were invited to on Friday night.

Changing the subject

Many men try to change the subject in a variety of ways if they don't want to discuss something:

> When something is bothering me and I am trying to talk about it, he'll say, 'I'm sorry,' (as if that settles it), then (briskly), 'Now let's talk about something more pleasant!' and proceeds to ignore any response I might have. This makes me see red – it is an aggressive act on his part, the way I see it. But if I say so or get upset, he says, 'I don't know what you're talking about. *I'm* not shouting, I'm not *fighting* like you.' Or sometimes he kisses me, hoping that will shut me up.

He will actually sit there and pick up the TV guide when we are talking and start reading it. It's unbelievable. When I complain, he says he doesn't know what I mean. Then he just turns the TV on to the channel he wants and starts watching.

He'll do anything to get out of the conversation: make a phone call, go to the fridge and look in it to see what he can eat, look through his diary. I wish he would just stop everything and talk to me until our conversation is over. I don't know how he can think that 'it will go away' if he ignores me. I mean, isn't it obvious that if someone needs to talk to you, the problem will remain unresolved until they *do* get a chance to talk about it?

Sometimes men deny that a problem exists at all – even while a woman is screaming that there is something wrong!

He was meeting my mother for the first time and I was nervous. He thinks it's fun to be rude sometimes, but I thought it's my Mum and all, and he must want her to like him. Well, he was *totally* awful, and behaved like a spoiled ten-year-old. I couldn't believe it. I was really upset but, later, when I tried to bring it up, he just looked at me from under the covers and said, 'Go to sleep, you're tired, I was fine, you're imagining all this.' He always says it's my problem if I'm upset, never admits that there's anything wrong, never that *he* might have been wrong. God forbid!

We were in the car and I was trying, for the umpteenth time, to talk to him about the way his best friend ignores me. It really hurts me that my boyfriend doesn't stick up for me over this, because the coldness of his friend is so obvious. But he still said, 'I don't know what you are talking about.' I was so frustrated by this that I grabbed the wheel and steered the car off the road. I almost crashed us! I did get his attention, but then we really had a fight, a huge one. It didn't do any good.

In addition to all this, if a woman insists on talking about the problem, a man will often tell her she is being 'petty'. Of course, this will only make her angrier, because his attitude is in itself a sign of condescension, and proof that he is not interested in what she is saying. He does not value the relationship enough to worry and wonder what it is that could be on her mind:

> We will sometimes have a huge fight in the morning before we go to work. Then we'll have to leave because we would be late. So I'm distracted all day and feel so sad and cry, dreading the moment when I have to go home. If I try to look at the argument objectively during the day, control my anger and try to see his side, we can sometimes have a productive argument and get beyond it. But by 5.30 he has usually decided to forget the fight and I'm left with all these things unsaid, feeling as though he doesn't even care enough to work through it.

'You're an idiot for saying I hurt you'

Another common response might be called 'irrational aggression', or 'bullying the person you just flattened'. In other words, another way men often try to shut women up is to attack the woman who is saying her feelings are hurt – just because they are hurt and she has the nerve to tell him about it.

In this self-righteous pattern, the man attacks the woman because she 'makes him feel guilty':

> We were on holiday, and he was not spending much time with me. He always preferred to be with his friend. I was hurt and beginning to feel very insecure. We were going to be visiting Paris, and I was excited by the idea of showing him around. I thought he had never been there. We had been talking about it a lot. Then, one night, he suddenly told me that he *had* been there before. I asked him who he had gone with and he told me it was with a girl he had been quite involved

with before me, the only one I felt jealous about. But he always made me feel like a psycho for feeling that way. Anyway, I said, 'Why didn't you tell me you had been to Paris?'

He got really mad, accused me of nagging, and started yelling at me, saying he didn't tell me because he 'knew I would react exactly like this' (jealous and insecure) and I was 'a drag'. He would rather lie to me than allow me to have momentary insecurity and comfort me through it.

Telling you what you feel is wrong

Another way some men shut a woman up is by telling her, after she has spoken, that her feelings are 'wrong' or 'incorrect':

> Whenever I tell him I am upset about something, if it isn't something *he* thinks is upsetting, he says, 'You shouldn't feel that way.'

> He says that if I feel bad about something, *I* should change the way I feel!

> He tells me I must be having my period or that I need a good fuck when I get upset. He is insinuating that it can't be the *real* me who is criticizing him, it must be due to a 'momentary female lapse of reason'.

Telling you you're crazy

Some men try to silence women by saying their thoughts and opinions are 'silly', 'crazy' or 'funny' and then can't understand why a woman may raise her voice in protest:

> My boyfriend always tells me I'm crazy when I get upset. He thinks any woman is crazy who gets really frustrated and shows it. He doesn't ever consider that there is a valid reason for how I feel.

> We were having one of our usual silent, resentful mornings after he had thoroughly upset, insulted and hurt me the night before. When I finally got up to leave

77

(I had to get out of there because he wouldn't talk and I couldn't stand that) he ran after me and called me a 'nut-case'. As if *I* was crazy to want to leave! Who wouldn't want to?

He has this habit of laughing or making what he thinks are witty remarks when I'm trying to talk about something serious or make a point, perhaps about politics. It makes me so angry, but if I tell him that, he asks why I'm so overly sensitive. 'Don't be a goose!' he'll say. I don't think there's anything he could do that could injure my dignity more or make me more resentful of him.

He has started to say, 'You need help,' whenever I am really upset. The thing is, I only get worked up into a tantrum because he won't listen to me or tries to belittle my feelings and shut me up. *That* is why I act 'crazy'. But he only sees the action, never the cause. So he says I should see a shrink so I can sort myself out, because it's 'obviously' nothing to do with him.

These kinds of clichéd reactions from men are emotionally violent. What is more, they carry with them the full weight of social disapproval of women's supposedly 'over-emotional' behavior. Why do men still plug into these stereotypes about women, or ridicule women's supposedly 'hysterical' or 'out of control' behavior?

All of these attitudes – silent indifference, ridicule and put-downs – cut off communication in a way which is very harmful to a relationship. They have the effect of putting the man in the position of power, as he seems to be saying that he doesn't have to bother with the woman's side of the story: 'Take it or leave it; I won't change.' So a woman is effectively faced with the choice of fighting back, leaving, or accepting the situation.

This refusal to listen and really talk things over used to have the effect of 'keeping a woman in her place', in the days when most women did not have independent incomes. Although the majority still earn much less than men, now that most women do have jobs outside the home, they have some possibility of leaving, and therefore more 'bargaining power' and more choices in this situation.

Of course, what women really want with the men in their lives is a two-way, respectful dialogue, and real emotional equality as this woman says so poignantly:

So far I've never found a man who would stop and sit with me and say, 'You're really upset about this. What is wrong? What can I do? Tell me if I hurt you and I will try to understand.' Even writing this makes me cry with frustration. My friends do that for me. Why can't he? It would be so wonderful to be respected like that.

THE PATTERN OF EVENTS DURING A FIGHT

This, then, is the pattern: home-grown male distancing (which puts the woman in the position of having to work to keep the emotional channels open), escalates into emotional battering or violence if the man reacts negatively to the woman's attempts to change the relationship, to make it more equal.

So, this is what women in the 1990s will face: as they try to make things work, humanize relationships, desire more equal emotional interaction, they will encounter unconscious resistance from many men, who do not see that what they are fighting to retain is not their 'male pride' but their dominance. This is part of the struggle to democratize the family that women have been engaged in throughout the twentieth century. It can be so frustrating and painful at times that many women may decide not to stay in relationships – that is is too hard, too difficult, too painful to try to get men to change, to listen and interact equally.

Indeed, the pattern of events *during* fights, once real fighting is underway, does not often encourage women to want to continue their relationships. Most women say that men continue to use the same emotionally violent tactics *during* the fight (not listening, ridiculing), that they did earlier, and so many women wind up screaming or crying, and feeling emotionally overwhelmed and traumatized.

Having you ever noticed any of the following infuriating tactics during a fight? If so, we hope that this analysis will help you get through them with a lot less pain!

Refusing to see your side of things

Too many men are still trying to use clichés such as 'Why don't you stop complaining?' and all the other psychological clap-trap of assumed male superiority to 'define' the situation and keep control of the relationship.

The 'I am right and you are wrong' style during a fight is no picnic:

> His expression seems to say, 'Why are you behaving this way? Making a scene. I have no idea what you expect *me* to do about it.'

Many men have special ways of aggravating the situation during a tense moment, by using gestures and phrases which send the message: 'You are being a pain in the ass. Irrational. What do you expect me to do about *your* problem?':

> He will say, 'I'm sorry *you're* upset,' in the most patronizing tone of voice, and then claim that he just apologized!

> He is very, very opinionated and his mind cannot be changed through logic, proof that he is mistaken, tears, shrieking, or anything else. Seldom is anything resolved. We don't talk anything over after a fight, just drift back together.

> It's always this condescending attitude of, 'Look, I know what you *think* I did, but you're wrong, I didn't do it, you're just imagining things.' Then if I insist that I know what happened, he just says, 'Look, you're wrong and I'm right. That's it. I don't want to discuss it any more.'

I get so exhausted at not being respected *ever* when I have a row with him. He always says I am wrong, my feelings are wrong, or even that what I am telling him he did is wrong – that he didn't even *do* it! It just makes me want to throw plates or go outside and scream for an hour. What I really want to do is punch him.

Compromise and trying to see another person's side of things is integral to the success of the relationship. This non-compromising, the-man-has-the-right-to-define-the-situation attitude makes women feel sad and alienated, because a true relationship is impossible.

My marriage was the most violent event in my life. It was short (three years) but I felt like I had lived ten years with him. We married very quickly, so I guess I never got to know him well enough. It wasn't the lack of money or the fact that we stayed home all the time that was hard. It was the complete lack of understanding of my feelings that he showed. It would frustrate me so much that I would start crying and then we would have a fight because my crying pissed him off no end. The thing I was originally upset about would be overlooked and we would get into these violent emotional scenes about my 'weakness' and 'neediness' and his distance and criticism. It just never got any further than that. We never even discussed the real problems.

Now I am without him, and although I sometimes get sentimental and miss him, I am amazed at how peaceful my days can be. I don't have that constant feeling that a bomb is about to go off.

Laughing at you

Just as women are frequently ridiculed for bringing up something that bothers them, they also often experience teasing, condescending remarks from men *during* an argument. The frustration and pain women feel when they are mimicked or teased by someone they love can be devastating – or infuriating:

I was standing there in the bathroom, crying my eyes out, and he was laughing at me, saying, 'You really are ridiculous. Look at the facts. You're being hysterical. I've never seen such an emotional display in my life.'

Everything I say when we are fighting is hilarious to him. He cracks up laughing, each thing I say is funnier and more stupid to him than the last. It is humiliating.

He says things like, 'Oh, boo-hoo-hoo, poor little girl.' I'd like to see how he would take it if *I* did such a thing to him!

This ridicule leads some women to apologize for the fight – even when they don't want to:

We had spent a fun day in the park sledding on the snowy hills with inner tubes from old car tires. We got home and I had a hot bath. He came in and said, 'Wasn't that fun? I'm going to give you that inner tube for your birthday.' I said, 'A rose would be nicer.' Well, it ended up being a big scene. We went out for dinner with some friends and when we came back he was sulking. He started saying that he couldn't believe I would refuse the inner tube for my birthday, that I was mercenary and ungrateful. He went on and on, cutting me off at every turn, proving each thing I brought up was wrong ... I ended up finding myself apologizing and agreeing that it had been very rude and unkind of me. I actually left that night thinking that! Then I got home and it dawned on me that I'd been wrapped around his little finger *again*.

Nasty fighting: trying to hurt the other person

In the last rounds of a fight the idea isn't to air grievances and reach an understanding, but just to wound the other person as deeply as possible:

Lying, while fighting, is dumb ... out of anger he lied and told me he'd been seeing another girl and had screwed her. I asked her name. He had to think a long time. A few months later I gently nudged her name into a conversation. He said, 'Who the hell is that? I've never heard of her!' Dummy! I feel lost when we fight. Very empty.

If I say he hurt my feelings by not calling, he says things like, 'You might ask your*self* why I don't call . . .' and so on, implying some vague nasty thing.

Of course, women as well as men can fight dirty. But men are more inclined to use any verbal weapon at hand to 'win', since men have been so heavily indoctrinated with the idea that a man must not let anyone step on his pride, he must never be 'wrong' – winning is all.

IS GOING TO BED REALLY MAKING UP?

The fight is over and it is bedtime. Now what? Are you going to have sex?

Women are often admonished not to take their fights to bed with them. But if a woman does go to bed with a man who is refusing to discuss something with her that matters to her and doesn't try to understand, then isn't going to bed with him capitulating?

Most women say that it is very important to them that problems and fights are not be dragged out over long periods of time – that the sooner they have talked it over, the better they feel. But what if the man refuses? Often by the time you're getting ready for bed, tension is still hanging in the air – at least for you. Should you 'take the fight to bed', or put it aside and not let it interfere with lovemaking? It is hard to feel like having sex if you feel disregarded or humiliated. However, many women in this situation say that they have been accused of 'withholding sex' to 'punish' and 'manipulate' the man:

When we fight and it gets resolved in a way where I feel heard and so does he, I am incredibly aroused and want him very much. But usually, I feel emotionally beat up (he doesn't, he got his way), and so he's very turned on. I hate going to bed with him like that. But I usually do, because I don't want to deal with what would happen if I said no. Then the fight would be re-enacted and I would be even more exhausted and humiliated.

A pattern has started with our fights now: they usually occur at night, just before bed. Then, after the fight, if I don't feel like sex (how could I?), he accuses me of punishing him. Then, sometimes, he'll pretend to give in and agree with me so he can get his way.

I connect sex with feelings. So when my feelings are hurt, I don't want sex. That seems logical to me, but I get hurt even more when I hear him tell me that it's 'just sex' and I 'shouldn't be so emotional about it'.

A woman can also find herself in the position of not wanting sex because of unresolved quarrels which have become a pattern. Even if the disagreements are small, the failures to resolve them can mount up, and a woman may feel less and less like sex.

This becomes 'ammunition' for some men to put women down once again. However, this is a valid way in which a woman can assert her own dignity and rights, by trying to be heard and get a resolution, so that she can continue the relationship as *herself*.

WHEN IT ALL BECOMES IMPOSSIBLE

One woman heart-rendingly describes her sadness resulting from the alienation she can't help but feel building up in her relationship with a man she dearly loves:

I want to be close to him, but I just can't, not like I was. He doesn't understand what I'm talking about, and goes really cold when I try to insist or explain. So now I have to try and forget and give up hoping he will change.

In other words, these patterns of fighting leave women in a no-win situation: if they can't have a dialogue with the man, it often seems they have to either accept him and things 'as is', or leave, as this woman describes:

> He never apologizes, just makes fun of me if I complain or get upset about anything. If I really insist, he just walks out. This puts me in an impossible position – what do I do, leave him? If I don't want to leave him, do I have to swallow my pride and never complain? This hurts my dignity, and affects my ability to handle the rest of my life well. (I work, etc.) Then I feel too upset or bothered by my unreleased or un-talked-about feelings with him to focus clearly on what I am doing. But if I let it out and scream, he looks at me like I am a 'nagging bitch' and still won't discuss the topic. So I am at a loss as to what to do. I don't know how to relate to him and still keep my sanity – but I don't want to lose him either.

Autocratic behavior leaves only black and white choices; a dialogue between equals would be so much better.

LIVING IN AN EMOTIONALLY VIOLENT ATMOSPHERE

Thus, one of the most common, yet unnamed, causes of fights in relationships is emotional battering or emotional violence. This is the background against which most relationships are lived. We have seen how these attitudes are built into language and 'everyday' behavior towards women, in ways which are apparently so small that to bring them up might lead to being accused of pettiness. Being placed in this frame of reference can create so much tension, defensiveness and discomfort that it is not surprising that women so often struggle to change their relationships, change the emotional dynamics, reshape the assumptions behind men's view of them. In fact, women are heroic in their attempts to refuse to be silenced and stereotyped.

And they are right: all of this can be changed.

PRODUCTIVE FIGHTING: TECHNIQUES FOR STAYING CLOSE

Fights can either be very harmful to a relationship, or they can lead to a positive airing of feelings that gets things back on the right track.

How can 'discussions' (fights) be more positive? Women often say they wish men would learn more of the 'female' skills of expressing warmth and closeness: how to pick up subtle clues from another person, how to be more empathetic and involved, how to respond to a request to talk something through. In short, women want men to learn to love not only sexually, but also emotionally.

These are just some of the values and attitudes that women told us they would like to see more of in men during fights:

> Be able to tell me exactly what you are feeling, as well as you can. And then be willing to listen without judging what I have to say. Try to put yourself in my place if you can.

> Never close a person off: don't refuse to talk or withdraw from a woman. It only makes things worse.

Changing the way you fight

Some women have managed to change relationships in which the man was not able to discuss issues into flourishing, happy and communicative ones, most often by seeing a counselor together.

Here, they describe the change:

> I like the openness we have now – the baring of ourselves to one another. It took a few years to be able to do this. He couldn't feel enough trust to be so vulnerable, but once he saw I wouldn't hurt him or use it against him later somehow, he opened up and was always 'there' for me . . . now we are both very happy.

> When there is a misunderstanding between us, we keep talking until we've both had our say. This

relationship means so much to both of us that we're prepared to talk things through until we're back on the right track.

Another woman chose a 'militant' route; by 'educating' her lover, she now has an equal and happy relationship:

In the beginning, he wouldn't do anything to help me around the house, he was just arrogant like most men, he expected me to do everything. So I had to make a big thing of making him see my point. If there were dirty dishes on the table, or dirty ashtrays, I just refused, for about a year, to move even a dish if he didn't also move a dish. If there were phone calls to be made, I just didn't make any, unless we stood right there together and he made just as many as I did. When he stopped, I stopped.

Now it is wonderful – he is so supportive and understanding, he helped me have a way to go back to work with the children here and he really takes a part in all the household. My sisters have both been married twice, it never lasts more than two years or three. I keep saying, 'Wait, wait! If you keep on trying, eventually you will have something great. Don't give up! Be really militant – *really*.' It is a shame that women have to do this to make men see, but it's worth it when you become a team and have that closeness.

To get fighting patterns to change can be difficult, because it is, in essence, a challenge to many men's whole idea of themselves: it is asking them to change their values, their stereotypes about women. But it can happen.

The best kind of fighting ends in a resolution in which each person comes to understand the other's point of view:

We don't fight. We resolve the problem. It feels great. We used to fight because I wanted to get every place on time, and we were always late because of him. We resolved the problem by deciding that for movies, plays, and concerts, we would be on time, because it's important. For dinner, gatherings and parties we are more lax about arrival time. Now he only feels pressured when it is important.

After a fight we both sit down and talk things out. We will then come to an understanding and cuddle up in each other's arms and fall asleep or make love.

Some couples have consciously made an agreement to try to avoid screaming, to discuss problems honestly, politely, and with kindness:

When we feel anger start to boil in us, we both sense it and we say to each other, 'Let's take a deep breath and try to be kind but honest.' Then we sit down or lie down and try to talk it through quietly. This way anger does get expressed, but not screeched. Screaming makes us both shut down and not hear, it is useless.

I express pretty much everything that I feel. I always have, and though I know this is basically good, I also have wanted to learn how to keep some things to myself and not come out with anything that happens to come into my mind. Doing that can hurt people, and sometimes turns right back on me. The man I am dating is quite closed, opposite to me. He is very respectful, and chooses his words carefully, always conscious of how I will feel about what he says. He has difficulty expressing 'negative' (his word) feelings, sometimes, though. I have helped him to feel free to do that, and he has helped me to bite my tongue some-times and not blurt out the first off-the-cuff thing I think of. Our communication is what I would consider very good!

We definitely have some juicy rows sometimes, but not that often. Mostly one or the other of us gets over-whelmed by work or something. He is so wonderful when I'm feeling that way – he never reacts badly or takes it personally. He usually gives me a hug and a massage or just a big, fat kiss and it makes me feel so much better! If he's being crabby, I try to do the same. Both of us can 'act up' at times, but we try to handle it with love and caring and it really works.

These situations are ideal! Don't they sound wonderful?

—4—

Should You Stay or Should You Go?

I know it's a terrible relationship, and it's not working.
I probably should leave, but I don't want to. I love him.

So many women have gone through long periods of asking
themsleves, 'Is it better to stay and try to change this
relationship if I can? Or should I leave?' In this chapter, we
will talk through all the questions one asks oneself when
reaching this decision.

ARE YOU HAPPY IN YOUR RELATIONSHIP?

One way to find out whether you want to leave or stay in a
relationship is to try this test:

1   Make a list of the qualities you have always wanted in a
man and a relationship. Do not think of your lover, just
make the list as if you had never met him.

2   List the qualities of this relationship or lover that you
want, and make another list of the aspects you don't want.

3   Compare the two lists.

4   Put the lists aside and ask yourself how you feel when
you are going to be seeing him soon. Are you excited,
tranquil, nervous? Are the feelings you have when you are
about to see him positive, do they enhance the quality of
your life?

5   In general, how do you feel when you walk away from him? Given that you may have had a fight or may have had a wonderful time, you can feel different on any particular day, but *in general*, do you have a feeling of well-being, that this love is worth whatever effort you put into it, a feeling of deep belonging?

6   How do you feel when you and your lover are with your friends? Are you proud to be with him? In social situations does he do things to make you feel secure and loved, or does he make you feel anxious and jealous?

7   Do you feel able to talk to him about anything? Or do you feel you are walking on eggshells every time you try to bring something up?

8   Do you wonder how he feels about you or does he make it a priority that you always know?

9   Are you satisfied with your sex life together? Do you feel beautiful and desirable with him? Does he tell you or show you that he loves you often enough?

10   Is it your love for him or his love for you that is giving you the most pleasure in the relationship?

In looking at your answers, do you think that you get *enough* of what you want? No one can give anyone everything, but are you getting at least, say, 70 per cent? What is your gut feeling? If you feel you are getting enough, go straight on to the next chapter!

DEFINING THE SITUATION

There are many cases in which it is clearly imperative for a woman to leave a relationship, for example, when her days are filled with emotional or physical violence.

But what about the borderline cases? The cases in which some things are bad and some are really good? It can be very difficult for a woman to weigh the love she feels against the reality of the situation. How important is happiness or stability? How strong are her feelings? What exactly are they: love (and which kind), hate (at times, at least), fear, fascination – even just not wanting to acknowledge defeat? How hard should a woman try to make it work?

This is the question for the 1990s: is the relationship you are in an equitable one? Or is it exploiting you, draining you emotionally or in terms of work? For the past few years, since the women's movement began calling for equal rights for women in the family, critics have been counterattacking by talking about the 'me' generation – labelling women 'selfish'. The latest media hype tells women that they can't 'have it all', they have to choose between career and family.

Yet men don't have to make this choice. Neither should women, except when caring for a newborn child – when men might stay at home too, In fact, the stereotype of women staying at home with the family is a pipe-dream: the great majority of women with children today work outside the home. This gives a woman independence: if a relationship is not fulfilling, why should she stay in it?

One of the most common reasons for staying is 'because I love him'. Whether a relationship is 'worth it' or not often comes down to this question: 'How much do I love him, and in what way?'

How do you love him?

One of the most confusing parts of being in an unsatisfying relationship is trying to work out exactly what you feel for your partner.

There are so many different kinds of love. One kind – the feeling of being 'in love' – is a classic part of the joy of being alive: luscious, exhilarating, unbounded:

The first time I went to bed with him, I felt as though the world had stopped and I was a shooting star sending out enough light to illuminate the blackest of black holes. Both in bed and out, it was an overpowering sensation and I couldn't get enough of him.

When I first saw him I felt a lurch, a leap, and then a kind of internal sigh, an, 'At last. Where have you been for so long?' A deep sense of recognition. It also felt scary as hell. He was like everyone I'd ever been in love with before in some small way and then himself, more so. He is beautiful to look at, astoundingly intelligent, very warm and beautifully sensual (but only in bed, almost never in public), his voice makes my ears feel good and my chest and spine, he has very penetrating eyes, his sense of humor is delightful, he can do or figure out almost anything, and he's maddening, frustrating, infuriating, invigorating, unpredictable, uncontrollable, and nice.

Both times I have been in love I've known it at once. The usual chatter that goes on in your head – which you more or less think of as yourself – suddenly seems much fainter and smaller, and underneath is something larger, quieter, more sure of itself.

Some women don't think it is worth staying in a relationship without this kind of love. As one woman puts it:

I can't imagine not loving totally, with abandon. It would be like being half alive, not really getting all you deserve. It would be a rip-off!

Caring or Passion?

But other women distrust this kind of love, and don't want to be in a relationship in which they are deeply 'in love'. They don't like the loss of control and the roller-coaster ups and downs. They find it all too painful and overwhelming – much too volatile and dangerous for true happiness:

Being in love can give pleasure, even joy, but most of the time it's painful, unreal and uncertain. It took a long time to learn anything from it, and most of what I learned is that I should avoid it.

I do not like being in love. I feel too vulnerable. I would rather be with someone I feel comfortable and safe with than be in love.

Being in love has its moments. The excitement is incomparable. But I do not like the hysteria, longing and inability to function.

These women prefer a more low-key love, one which leaves time and energy for a broader spectrum of interests – work, friends, children and so on:

I've been 'in love' in the passionate way you see in movies and read about in books, and it took too much from me. My friends and my career are very important to me, and I had nothing left for them when I was 'in love'. I prefer now to have nice relationships with nice men – my life is my own.

Being really 'in love' is all-consuming. I found it sucked me dry. I learned to avoid it, because I don't like that feeling. I was a complete wreck, and only thought about him. The rest of my life fell apart.

I always thought that love was a feeling that would descend upon me from the heavens – I had no control over it and I had to roll with the punches. But now I am involved with a man who did not sweep me off my feet at first. He was just a nice, respectful, affectionate guy. And I grew to love him, chose to love him. We argue sometimes, but he treats me as an equal, and is always thinking of me and of ways to show me his love, and I do the same. We have created a haven of love and warmth, and there are no explosive scenes. I don't miss crying all night, waiting for phone calls, for apologies, wondering where he is, wondering where 'it' is going. This is the kind of love I want.

Many women choose to have less intense relationships – relationships that are loving but not too intense – at various times in their lives. Choosing a relationship *only* because you know it will be 'smooth' and straightforward can mean missing out on some exhilarating experiences. But for some

women soothing relationships can sometimes be exactly
what they want and need:

> I went out with a couple of guys who were really sweet
> but with whom I felt no fire or excitement. This was
> after a year in a relationship that wore me out
> emotionally. For a while, these men were great. It
> soothed my battered heart.

Others believe that women who like a caring kind of love
are more 'mature' than those who want the excitement of
passion. it can be argued both ways. Are those who leave
relationships which are lacking in passion living more fully
– not 'settling'? Perhaps in the past when many of us were
totally dependent economically, we were forced to choose
'a good provider' rather than follow our hearts. But most
women say they do not believe this; they believe that
choosing carefully, rationally, is the better part of wisdom.

But in the end, why make judgements? All the forms of
love are valid; which we prefer depend on what we want
from a relationship at a given time in our lives.

Interestingly, while people usually say there are only two
different types of love – being passionately 'in love', or
being nurturing and caring (usually, learning to care over
time) – generally, women's descriptions of their feelings do
not exactly fit these neat categories. Most women say that
passion, or passionate love, means feeling not only
physical passion but also emotional passion, and often they
say that one cannot exist without the other. The body/mind
split that is so prevalent in Western society is not one that
emerges in women's descriptions of the feelings they call
'love'.

Is not loving 'enough' a reason to leave?

Some women carry a secret guilt for not being enough in
love with their mates, not 'wildly in love':

> What about when he loves you – you know he loves
> you, even though he may not give you just what you

want – what then? Should you leave? Do you have the right to leave? He hasn't done anything wrong, after all.

What if you don't love him 'enough' (how much is that)?

I have found a man who gives me all the love, nurturing, support and strength that I always wanted, but he is not a 'bad boy' like my previous lovers. This results in my not having the same kind of wild passion for him that I had with other men. I sometimes wonder if I should stay in this relationship if I don't have a crazy and passionate feeling towards him.

I'm seeing this 'nice' guy who is sweet and loyal. It's very un-dramatic and nothing ever really happens. I feel embarrassed to say this, but I'm bored. Although there are none of those ups and downs that I had when I was married, this is too much the reverse. It doesn't feel good; I thought it would be a solution, to find someone I could grow to love . . . but it's boring, and unsatisfying.

One woman celebrates leaving a boring, unfulfilling marriage:

I can't believe I spent all that time in a marriage that was so empty. I never had fun with my husband. I guess I never thought you could have fun with a man. Now I know I'm wrong – my lover and I have a ball together! We spend a lot of time in bed, talking and enjoying each other's bodies. He really appreciates me and shows me in lots of ways. I'm so glad I found this and didn't spend my whole life lonely in a marriage bed.

Pressure to give more than you've got

Another feeling women sometimes describe is living with a vague feeling of not giving enough, a feeling of semi-disapproval or disappointment coming from the man, who feels he is not getting enough attention, that the woman never has enough time 'for him'. One woman answered this unspoken accusation in the following way:

> You are assuming my function is to serve you – and therefore always have a vague bitchy attitude or pout when I'm doing something else – even when I'm working! *Especially* when I'm working! You think all my time and attention should be focused on *you*!

Are you constantly criticized, or criticizing yourself, for not spending enough time with him? So many women now have full-time jobs that one of the most pressing concerns women face is how to deal with men's assumption that women should always be there for them. Most men turn to women for comfort and attention, to make life 'civilized': they believe we should dress nicely for them, listen to them, be ready to go out with them whenever they want. (Was life ever like that, given the enormous amount of work women have always done in the home?) Today it is certainly impossible for a woman to be a full-time support person, especially to someone who does not reciprocate that support.

Unequal emotional support

We have seen how a lot of women are doing all the 'emotional upkeep' in a relationship. Women are trained to please others, and men in particular.

Do you find yourself constantly worrying about pleasing your partner? One woman describes this state of mind:

> Like him, but I also like to have time alone, sometimes I like to sleep alone – not always feel pressure to be "sexy" or ready for sex if he wants it, to be friendly and charming. There are a lot of nights when I come home from work so wiped out that the thought of sex just doesn't interest me, but I have it anyway, because I don't want to make him think I don't find him attractive.

We can become so involved with trying to figure out how to please, or make the other person emotionally comfortable, that we forget to watch out for our own needs. We think, 'How much can I give?' not, 'I need him to nurture all my resources so that I can reach the goals I have set for myself.' We are used to putting men first.

Thinking it through

Usually there is no one incident that tells a woman she had better get out of a relationship, more often it is a series of incidents, a constant feeling of being emotionally in suspense, or the same serious problems recurring. But, as these kinds of relationships gradually take their toll, battering and eroding your morale, it is easy to lose touch with how much it is really costing to continue, and make a wrong decision.

Married women often spend several years of anguish debating whether to leave a marriage before deciding to get a divorce; they later say, on the whole, that they were far more unhappy during this period of trying to deciding than during or after the divorce.

In the same way, women in half-good/half-bad relationships can go through utter agony, trying to work out what to do:

Some days I think I cannot go on one more minute, I feel so sad. And other days I can't imagine leaving him, I love him so much. I always love him, but sometimes I wonder if that is enough. I don't know what to do.

He has never done one big thing, like sleep with someone else, or forget my birthday or something. It's just all these 'little' things, always this feeling of waiting for the other shoe to drop, never knowing what kind of a day we will have together. I don't know whether I love him or not anymore. I just don't know.

When we started having scenes and I realized that I was crying two or three times a week because of fights we had, I remember thinking, 'Why am I staying?' But

I loved so much about him and my feelings went so deep that I couldn't leave just because things were rough. I had to wean myself away very gradually.

When he does something nice, I think, 'See, he really does care, we really are in love, everything's really fine, remember this the next time things go wrong with him.' And then the next day, when he does something really mean and rotten, I think, 'This is how it *really* is, most of the time.' And I know that it's true. I love him madly. I wonder what I should do at this point.

I knew when we fell in love that we would not have a smooth relationship, because he is a very temperamental man. But I'm not the kind of person who needs to 'conform', or have a 'model home' type of relationship. So it didn't bother me. At least, it didn't used to. But at this point, I can't quite think of one reason that I should stay in this relationship. On the other hand, I can't really bring myself to break it off, even though everything that is going on right now is bloody awful.

AGONIZING CHOICES: WHEN IT'S REALLY FIFTY-FIFTY

Borderline good/bad relationships are hard to work out. Part of you may say, 'No matter what, no matter how bad it is, the feeling that he *does* want me, he *does* love me, is so strong that I can't be wrong!' The belief in this feeling, or the memory of it – even just the longing for that feeling – is hard to resist. Especially when your self-esteem is wilting from bad treatment. So, the worse things get, the harder it becomes to give up the belief that 'underneath it all, he loves me. He says so, I know it's so, and he will come through, just as soon as he's over this difficult period.'

He may indeed love you in his way. But if this relationship is continually disappointing you or hurting you, then what can you do? In most cases, it is better to leave, unless some drastic changes can be made.

One of the best ways to think clearly is to spend a week or two alone, away from him, re-orienting your life – seeing friends or working on projects you especially like. After a few initial cramps of pain, you will find your equilibrium returns, and you can begin to think more clearly about what should be done.

How hard is it to tell him you want to get away and have time alone? It can be very difficult because you may fear his reaction, and, on a deeper level, you may hate giving up his love. However unsatisfying it may be, there are probably times when it is (or was) great; the memory of that can make it difficult to accept that the 'bad' part is the reality now and will continue to be.

Even harder to give up than his love for you may be your love for him. Leaving him doesn't necessarily mean you must stop loving him and won't miss him. Obviously, no one can stop loving someone in one minute. But as well as being upset, you probably feel a good deal of anger at things that have happened. Acknowledging your anger is crucial; this is a key which can unlock hidden strength and great inner resources. Feminists have pointed out how much of women's depression (for which we are prescribed millions of tranquilizers) is anger turned in on ourselves. This is certainly true – and there is no better time for remembering this than during the 'depressed' and agonizing moments of contemplating breaking off or radically redefining a relationship.

THE STAGES OF LEAVING

The process of leave-taking (whether emotional or physical) usually happens in stages. First women bargain with themselves: 'OK, so I won't ask him to do the laundry or wash the dishes anymore – it's not worth it. I love him, he's a man and you just can't expect all this overnight, but I can enjoy him – and where else could I find a better lover, or a man who loves me as well?' When even this bargain doesn't really work, next to go is a woman's belief that she *is* loved. Still, she may stay because, 'I still love how well we know each other, what we have built up over time, and I hope he believes in this too . . . ' and so on.

With each bargaining chip in this interior dialogue a

woman gives up more and more of her dreams, and denies more and more of her needs, until she may feel emotionally very alone. As she struggles she may feel that she is giving more than he is emotionally, trying harder to make it work: 'Why doesn't he seem to want to meet me half-way? Does he even understand that he is not? Will the relationship ever be better? Am I a fool to continue it? Should I keep on struggling? Give less energy to it? Should I *leave*?'

Double lives: leaving emotionally

In order to deal with unsatisfactory or half-satisfactory relationships, many women lead double lives emotionally, staying in their relationship, but limiting the part of themselves they risk exposing to their lover. They find they channel more and more of their emotional energy into friends, children and their work.

One woman describes how she has come to handle her relationship:

> I just don't focus so much on it any more. Then if I am disappointed, it doesn't matter so much. Maybe the love will build back up over a period of time. If not, it's better to have other parts of my life I am involved in. Then everything goes smoother.

Most women separate themselves emotionally in these cases without really ever trying; it just happens. They find themselves drifting away, no longer able to relate so fully to the other person, who does not seem to see them or what is happening. They find they are not as close as before, that they automatically hold part of themselves back. As one woman describes it:

> The relationship doesn't mean as much as it once did. It's peripheral to my life now, because I have grown and changed and he has not.

This emotional alienation can also express itself sexually. If a woman is offering her real self and her true feelings, and is constantly hurt, a pattern will usually be established: she gradually wants sex less and less as she becomes less emotionally involved in the relationship. Often, at this point, the man starts to complain that there is not enough sex and may begin looking elsewhere. This leads to further distance and alienation (which the woman may struggle at times to break through, as seen in Chapter 3).

When women leave sexually and emotionally, without actually removing themselves from the scene, the question they often ask is, 'Do I want to stay in this relationship and compromise, accept getting less out of it than I wanted, the kind of love I dreamed of, or should I leave and begin my life again?'

Quite a few delay leaving, because they doubt whether another relationship would be different.

> My kid is twelve and having a lot of problems adjusting to life without his Dad. I know it's better for both of us this way, but things happen that make me wonder. Like the other night, my boyfriend started accusing me of coming on to a man I work with. It turned into a ridiculous row that ended up nowhere. My son was watching from upstairs and got all upset and started crying. Eventually I got him tucked in, and John and I went to bed in silence. I lay there and thought, 'See, you thought it would be different after you divorced Dan, but the same thing is happening now. Is it me? Why is this happening? It wasn't this way in the beginning.'

Other women delay leaving because they don't want to to go through the pain:

> I know that this relationship isn't making me happy, but I just can't bear to go through the pain again of separating my life from someone, of starting over. My divorce was so hard, and I just don't want to do it again. Even though I'm not feeling fulfilled, I think it might be less painful to stay than to leave.

WHEN YOU LEAVE, EVEN THOUGH YOU STILL LOVE HIM

Leaving a relationship is never easy. Listen to one woman's decision to force herself to stay away and what her reasons are:

> What is there to do? Last night, whilst I was out, my 'friend' (my lover) called, very distressed, apparently, about the distance that has developed between us. I am distressed too. But the closeness of the relationship would only be possible for me if he was to change. If I would try to carry the relationship, accepting him as he is, I would explode with indignation, take revenge on him for everything that I had accepted in demure affection for the sake of the truly wonderful moments we are able to share. That way I would eventually kill the potential of these moments happening between us. Then I would have to withdraw because there would be nothing to stay for. So, to preserve what I love I must withdraw now.
>
> I must withdraw for the sake of my belief in a real – or what I call real – relationship, because I must grow more and more to become myself, to be able to respond to other people with all my potential, if I want to have a chance to meet the person with equality – if ever I should meet the person with whom it is possible to fulfill my belief. I believe you have to learn to treasure all you have and not go beyond the line of what you honestly can treasure. If that means that I have to live more remote from another human being than I wish to do, then that is the better pain to take into the future.

And two others:

> I look at him across a crowded room or in the cab that he drives and I see such beauty, a man I love so much. But the things he says to me, the criticisms and denegration of my character and integrity are taking their toll. I just can't pretend that I am happy any more.

I'm so tired. It's a constant, incessant disappointment – I *live* in disappointment. It's crushing my optimism and hope about life. I have to leave, but the thought terrifies me. I wish so much that it could be what I thought, and what I wanted it to be.

I didn't realize how this relationship was affecting me – I haven't been aware of the way it has eroded my sense of self and my attitude towards life. But I have been doing a lot of talking with my friends, and now I know I have to make the break. It's going to be hard. But I can't do anything else, he won't change, he's told me so.

Some of the saddest statements come from women who are saying goodbye to those they love. Listen to this woman's letter to the man she was leaving:

I love you so much. Our problem has nothing to do with my friends, as you claim. You are so proud and try to make me feel so lousy that I don't want to share them with you. You want me to be just like Jean, someone who grimaces when asked if she is still with Jim – someone who allows for so much hurt and being walked on so much – you think that's a wonderful woman. Well, that is a wonderful woman (there are many things I like about her), but that's a stupid woman too. If you think that's what a relationship should be, then we have very different ideas about that.

I tried every way I know to be everything I wanted to be for you, and it hasn't been enough. I have a body and a brain many men would love to have as their own, but you reject them time and time again, while lusting after or making passes at God knows who (plus one of my dearest friends). I feel many conflicting emotions about it, but mostly I wonder, *why*? I've always been there for you, loving you, loving your brain, loving your cock, caring and trying to help you and myself be the best we can be together. Trying to hold the team

104

together. But I can't do it alone. I can't live with you, knowing things go on, like your making a play for Laura after I've gone to work. I mean, what is the *reason*? I have been trying to fulfill you for eighteen months and I feel like I'm bruised and battered from being for our team all alone and beating my head against a brick wall.

I love you desperately, but there is nothing I can do anymore except drown with you, or take some action. I need to be loved, wanted, to know someone really thinks I'm gorgeous sometimes, who gives me his undivided attention sometimes. I've lost all that feeling with you, and I need it desperately. You must realize how you need it too, and then see how I do. You require so much sexual attention that having a woman (whom others would want) living with you and delighting so excessively in your boner isn't even enough for you! You require so much emotional attention that your friends have to make up for all the love and attention you seem to need from me and don't think you're getting! Christ! Then I am chastized for crying in the mornings and dreaming of evenings with you when you ravage me and we eat dinner and completely lose ourselves in each other. How can you reprimand me for wanting that? My God, are you a fool? That is the *best*! Don't you remember?

There is no law written that that has to end. And there's no reason why I should be told that I'm a pessimist and a fatalist if I say I don't think it will ever come again. Because I *do* believe it should, but I don't believe you can right now. Or you won't.

So let me go – love me enough to set me free from this thing and live while you work it out. I love you and want to feel that that is something you treasure again. Until then, I have to keep it inside because I can't give it to you any more. Not until you really want it – in the right way – and are willing and able to grab it by the balls with me and do it.

ARE YOU AFRAID TO LEAVE?

If you are in a bad relationship, and don't want to leave, ask yourself why. Clarify your thoughts by making a list of what you are getting out of it. Is he interesting? Sexy? *Sometimes* very understanding? Make a list of your fears, too.

Are any of the following your reasons for staying?

- I won't find anyone else.

- I won't find anyone else as good, interesting, sexy, etc.

- He's more special than anyone I've ever met. (Why?)

- This is my last chance because of my age.

- I've already invested so much time, I can't give up now.

- I don't think people should leave other people.

- He says he loves me, and even though he acts appallingly sometimes, I believe him. I feel it's true.

- His love is more important to me than another love could be because —.

- I like the social approval of having a partner.

- I don't like being 'single' or without a partner.

It is important to remember that if you answer yes to any of the above, you need not be too hard on yourself.

On the other hand, it is important to ask yourself whether you have become debilitated, unable to judge your own situation and not strong enough to look for a way to get your own needs met. Are you always putting your own needs on the back burner, while things get 'straightened out', or you 'help him'? The imbalance of power many men set up in relationships typically leads women to ask themselves, 'Is *he* feeling all right? Does he still love me? What is *his* mood today?' not, 'Do I feel all right? Do I want this kind of relationship?

One women recalls her own experience of not being strong enough to leave, to take her own needs seriously enough:

I spent a year with him. For three quarters of that year I was unhappy. For a while I was willing to put up with the sadness because he meant so much to me. But I didn't keep in touch with my friends. I was sloppy at work, and my health suffered. I was lucky enough to have good friends who were careful to be supportive of my desire to be with him and at the same time gently showed me that my life and my own sense of self-worth were being decimated by the relationship. I got to the point where I was ready to consider their side of things, where I was ready to see that the good no longer outweighed the bad. What I was getting from the relationship was not enough to compensate for the amount that was being taken from me.

'I left, but it was premature. I wasn't ready to let go of him. I still saw value in what we shared together, and couldn't bear never to see him again. So, after a couple of weeks of incessant calling and visiting from him, I gave in and went back. Six months later, the problems were even worse than the last time.

Finally, I had had it. I spent a couple of months talking about it to my friends, about what kind of relationship I wanted and what kind of relationship I was in – and the incongruity between the two. I realized that he would never change in the ways I needed him to (even having let go of some of my less important needs, I still knew this would be true about the remaining ones), and I could not be happy in the relationship the way it was.

That winter was very hard. I really never thought I would be able to leave, I didn't think I could bear the pain, couldn't stand to think about being without him, him being with someone else, me being with someone else, all those thoughts. But I drew on the strength of my friends and what I knew in my heart of hearts was right for me. I couldn't compromise myself any more, couldn't stand to watch myself disappear any longer. So I left.

MAKING THE BREAK

There comes a point at which many women can no longer deny the overwhelming need they have to get out of a relationship – no matter how hard this may be psychologically, financially or socially.

These women explain what helped them make the decision to leave:

I was told to try making lists of the pros and cons of the relationship. I resented this, thinking it unromantic and too practical, but I was so unhappy that I had to do something. So I tried it and it really helped. I made a list of the good things with us, and the bad things. Then I made a list of what I really wanted, and a list of what I was getting. When I saw it on paper, and it wasn't running around in my head, all jumbled up, I was able to think more clearly and made a decision.

I bounced everything off my friends. I had bottled things up for a long time, so this helped me in two ways: I got things out, and I got their advice. I also felt I had crossed a line, I was not 'his' any more.

I gave up trying to talk to *him* about it and started talking to others about it. The men that are my friends were a great help, because they happen to be the kind of men I would like my lover to be. And I asked them about the way they treat women as lovers, the way they speak to them, things they do for them, ways they love them. And the answers made my heart break, because they were the things I always wanted to hear him say about me but he never did. I had repressed those desires so as not to be disappointed. Hearing them from my friends gave me a strong dose of reality, the bad reality of my relationship.

I started to fill my life up with other things. I didn't want to, I wanted to just lie around and wait for his call, wait for him to tell me whether we were going to do any thing that day/week/year, wait for him to 'come through' – but, instead, I made other plans, went to the movies, saw more friends. I even flirted a little! After a few weeks of this, I was detached enough to decide I could live without him.

LEAVING WITH THE LEAST PAIN

One day at a time

The concept of 'one day at a time' has helped a lot of people get over various problem relationships: relationships with drugs and alcohol, food, people, money. This credo works very well when breaking up with a man. It is tempting to sentimentalize the past and rekindle hope for the future when you are feeling a lot of pain and miss someone, even when you know you want to leave him. If you can think only of today, not yesterday or tomorrow, it is remarkable how quickly you will find the days add up, and the healing will come. As one woman said:

> At first I worried, if I leave, will I really have something better? I learned the answer was, 'Yes! Myself! I will have myself back!'

Most women say the worst part is before they make the decision to leave; after that it is much easier. And one *does* get beyond the feelings:

> When someone told me then that one day I would say 'John who?' I thought they were crazy and shallow. I thought they didn't know a thing about love, about passion, about pain. But they were right. Today I feel completely secure in my decision to leave, feel no regret, only gratitude to myself for realizing I wasn't getting my needs met and doing something about it, and to my friends for helping me through it.

Don't talk to him

Many women say that the way to leave is to have absolutely no contact with him whatsoever. This may seem extreme or overly dramatic, but it is important.

Immediately after you've summoned up enough strength and courage to leave a man, you usually feel very

109

vulnerable. There is a fragile side to every person that is naturally heightened at a time of wrenching away from a lover, no matter what has transpired. As one woman puts it,

> It's as if you're a walking wound, and anything that happens can feel like salt being thrown at you, even if someone on the street is mean or something. Things that normally would just irritate you are suddenly absolutely horrible!

This is by no means meant as a definition of women as wounded victims; it is also a painful and vulnerable experience for many men. The point is to treat yourself especially well when you are breaking up, and not to get impatient with yourself for being emotional. It is only natural.

No communication means:

● Not reading letters, old ones or new ones.

● Not answering phone calls. A phone call or a letter from the man you are leaving will probably only make you feel even less happy, less convinced of your own decision, and less able to stick to your priorities.

● If the flowers come, throw them out or give them to someone.

● Give all your photographs of him to a friend for safekeeping. They might be fun to have some day, but right now they are an emotional minefield that you don't need to negotiate.

● Ask friends you have in common not to mention him to you if they can help it, and don't indulge your own curiosity. Knowing where he was last night, or who he was with, will probably only be upsetting.

● Avoid going to old haunts, or that favorite restaurant. Promise yourself you can go back in a year; by then you won't want to!

● On special anniversaries, like the first time you slept with him, make plans to be with very good friends – or even your new lover!

Realize that this is only limiting your life for a little while. It is not a permanent situation. These feelings *are* going to pass, even though you may feel they won't. And your life will again be your own; you will again take charge.

Go out with another man?

Even though it might be the last thing in the world you feel like doing, it could be helpful to go out on a few dates, as this woman found:

> The idea of going out on a date when I left him made my stomach turn. The idea of *men* made my stomach turn. I couldn't bear even kissing one. But my girl-friend said, 'I know you don't want to do this, but go out with John tonight.' She got me dressed up and did my face and I went. And I had a terrific time. I didn't kiss him or anything, but for five hours I got a lot of great attention, and it soothed my bruised ego and heart and did more for me than anything else.

See your women friends

When you are exhausted from trying to make a relation-ship with a man work and think nothing can make you feel better, it's amazing how energizing it can be to get together with your women friends (see also Chapter 7).

> After I broke up with him, I asked all my women friends over to dinner. We ate like pigs, drank cham-pagne, laughed, cried, and it was one of the best nights of my life. They helped me get through so much, I wanted to thank them.

> Women are the most important people in my life. My close relationships with women have kept me going when all else failed.

> She has helped me go through childbirth, divorce, depression. Every time I've needed a helping hand, she's been there.

I always feel great after I see her because we talk about everything so easily. She has helped me through innumerable difficult times and I love her very much.

RECOGNIZING YOUR ANGER

An important part of leaving and being able to say goodbye to all the feelings is to recognize and express not only sadness (if you are sad) but also anger. Whether you decide to express this anger with the man in question, or with a friend or counselor, this will help keep the anger from turning around on you and making you feel confused, guilty, depressed or 'worthless'. Anger is not a 'bad' emotion; it is, however, one that women are usually told they have no right to feel. But we do have the right, and it is important to acknowledge it, to *say* that we have not been treated well.

One woman describes this very clearly:

By the end of the relationship my anger became a source of strength for me. Realizing it and holding on to it was one of the most empowering feelings I ever had. You always learn that 'ladies shouldn't get angry', and 'if you can't say something nice about (to) someone, say nothing at all'. Well, that's crap. When I was able to really realize the anger I felt towards him, I was able to express it to myself and friends and this propelled me through leaving him. When I felt myself beginning to weaken, I would tap into it and it gave me hope, energy and determination about the change I was making.

USING THE BREAK AS A MAJOR OPPORTUNITY

Most women feel very good after finally making the break, as this woman describes:

I spent the second year of our relationship living in the past, remembering how good it was in the beginning.

Things were going really badly, he became very cold and distant. On one occasion I planned a lovely second-anniversary dinner for us, spent all day running around looking for just the right kind of steak, the best wine, the perfect candles, and he never turned up! He was busy getting a tan at the beach. That night I lay in bed trying to sleep and remembering how he used to say to me, 'I'm so in love with you, I can hardly eat!'

The final break came after one morning when I dropped by his flat on the way to work with a bunch of flowers, and he was in bed with someone. I threw the keys down on the bed and walked out.

I spent the next two weeks at a friend's house, someone he had never met. I holed up there and spent time with her and other friends, keeping away from him. His best friend had a spare key, and, while he was away one weekend, I went in and got all my things.

Leaving him was the best thing I ever did. I was unhappy for so much of the time I was with him, and didn't realize (or forgot!) that life can be so much better than that. I had forgotten how to laugh, how to wake up on a Saturday morning and look forward to the weekend, alone, with friends, or with my family. Now I laugh, and look forward to coming home to my warm flat, doing nice things for myself, travelling, going out on dates – I feel I have sprouted wings. I own myself again.

All the things you never had time for, or were too depressed to do, or always meant to do 'when you had time', do now! They can be small things: taking bubble baths, buying make-up if you can afford it, enjoying sports, taking yourself to the movies, getting lots of sleep, renting a funny video (chances are you have not laughed much lately). Or, it can mean starting a major new project, a job search or a serious hobby that you have been putting off but have dreamed of for half your life. Take steps now and do it.

Changing your life, re-orienting your life – what a great

opportunity! You can do *anything*. How many times are there in life when you can be so free, have so many options? You have 'lost' something, but you have also gained. You have got *yourself* back, you have and gained a chance to review all parts of your life. Do you like your job? Where you live? Your friends? What major goals in life have you put aside? Use this time to your advantage. Explore the world! Re-invent things for yourself in daring new ways! You'll never regret it.

The Good Stuff

___

After all this, you may be wondering if there is anything good left. Well, never fear! Although the 1970s and 1980s have been full of conflicts, in the 1990s we're going to be able to enjoy the good part of our relationships – with no guilt!

CELEBRATING THE GREAT TIMES

Women love to talk about all the great times they have in their relationships.

Most of us can think of a particular way of spending time together, or a mood, that is happy, and very precious:

> You know what I like? I like noodling around the house in my oldest clothes on a Saturday morning, mumbling together with him (in his old clothes, too, or his ancient terry-cloth bathrobe), gradually waking up, looking in the refrigerator, picking up last night's dishes, looking out the window, deciding if we want to take the dogs out for a walk.

> When I'm washing my hair, it takes for ever. Sometimes he keeps me company while I do it, or shampoos it for me – how I love that! Then he sits and talks to me while I dry it. What a doll.

> I love weekends where we never get out of bed for a whole day. We wake up and make love. Then we eat breakfast, watch a movie, and go back to bed. All

afternoon we watch TV, snack, make love and nap. It's best when it's raining outside. We unplug the phone and disappear from the world altogether.

I love going out with him. He's fun, and so exciting. When he calls me and says he's coming over, I get butterflies in my stomach. I get dressed thinking how he will react when he sees me, thinking how he will like how I look. The whole time I am smiling, excited to be seeing him. When he comes in the door, he always hugs and kisses me, and I love the smell of his leather jacket mixed with his cologne as he presses up against me. Then, usually we take a cab and go out to eat. He holds my hand and kisses me during dinner. I'm so happy – This has been going on for about six months.

I like to shower with him, watch the water fall along his long, strong legs and across his shoulders, watch him lather soap all over his hairy chest and arms, all over his penis. Sometimes I give him oral sex under the hot water! He loves to do the same to me, or sometimes he bathes me in the tub with bubbles, and masturbates me at the same time. Wow! I could keep that up for hours. I usually come two or three times. When I get out of the bath, my fingers are all shriveled up from being in the water so long! Sometimes we get so wild, we are exhausted and can hardly make it out of the bathroom!

I can be with him scrambling over stones to cross a river or clambering up some beach cliffs and feel totally at peace with him and with myself and with the world around me. I can feel how he is in the same trance of peace and contentment in the way he notices with loving interest little happenings in the water or amongst the grass.

Are these the same women we heard in Chapter 1? How can they sound so different?

The men women describe here are indeed the men who at other times are distant and silent, or exhibit other 'male' distancing patterns discussed earlier. Most relationships are mixed; there are the good parts and the not-so-good parts. Even though women may be having some of the problems we saw earlier in the book, most also find many things they cherish and enjoy in their relationships.

SHOULD YOU FEEL GUILTY IF IT'S NOT PERFECT?

Do you have a right to enjoy the good stuff if your relationship isn't great, or if there are terrible problems, no matter how 'in love' you are?

Women are generally thought to be 'masochists' if they are in a problematic relationship. This atmosphere of social disapproval is so heavy that many women harbor a secret fear that 'I shouldn't really be enjoying this – he screamed at me yesterday and said the most disgusting things. No woman in her right mind should be treated that way. If I let myself enjoy these kisses he is offering me now, it must mean I accept the relationship, including the insults. But I *do* like what he is doing now. Am I hopeless? Is this a loss of my integrity?'

Perhaps you only enjoy the sex and the affection but little else in your relationship. Maybe you think he's a great guy, but he really doesn't have a clue about *you* – or how to have an equal relationship with a woman. Say you really like the places he finds for you to go together, but you find it hard to talk to him (at least, much harder than talking to your women friends).

Does this mean you shouldn't be in the relationship? That you have hidden, nefarious motives? Are you just bending to pressures that imply you are 'nothing without a man'? Are you wrong to 'pig out' on the good parts if there are bad or inadequate parts?

Although most of us realize that no relationship will ever be perfect, we are constantly bombarded with the ideal of everlasting bliss, as this woman describes:

I was raised with the idea that my permanent relation-ship would be one where romance flourished every single second of the day. I would be permanently

117

attracted to my mate, and nothing would ever get us down, we would live on love, and I would feel like a queen every day of my life after I married him. Oh, and we would never fight – if we did, it meant that it was a 'bad' relationship.

There is an assumption in our society that if a relationship is not 'perfect', first the woman is to blame; second, she should leave; or third, she must be masochistic or neurotic if she stays. This leaves us with little option but to tell everyone that things are fine, every minute of the day (and night) – or to leave.

BEING REALISTIC: RELATIONSHIPS IN THE 1990s

But what about the reality? Many of us have found relationships with men we love – relationships that are not perfect, but that definitely have something worthwhile and some very happy moments. Are we 'unliberated' to stay in them?

To be realistic, if you choose to stay in a relationship with a man, you are probably dealing with some of the problems we have outlined in this book – problems that society says don't exist (the only 'problem' is you: *you* 'love too much' or *you* are 'confused' or 'selfish', or 'your expectations are too high' – or something!).

But why blame yourself? Why be so hard on yourself? You are living in an historical period in which relationships are undergoing tremendous change. Throughout the twentieth century, and increasingly now, women are trying to democratize the family and their relationships with men. Most men have yet to fully comprehend and adjust to the changes. Should we give up relationships with men because of this? (And aren't parts of ourselves also in conflict, aren't we still thinking through what all this means?)

No, of course we need not give up relationships, but it *is* very important to try to see clearly the dynamics of what is going on. The dynamics set in motion by the assumed emotional contract, as seen in Chapter 1, can be harmful to women, if allowed to go unquestioned, unchecked. Clarifying what is going on, pinpointing the hidden patterns that can be so damaging, is what we are doing together in this book.

WOMEN ARE NOT 'MASOCHISTS' IF THEY STAY IN IMPERFECT RELATIONSHIPS

There is great pressure on women to be 'successful' in their personal lives – which means to be 'happy', 'stable' and eventually get married. Women are often put down if they are in a relationship that is not like that:

> I love my boyfriend very much, but we fight a lot – too much; I am trying to change this. I get so sick of people asking me why I stay, why I don't give up. 'I love him,' I say! They think if it's not perfect, I should leave. I'm tired of being put down by them.

Usually, unhappy relationships do not start out badly; often they begin with intense attraction and emotional involvement, so that later, when the man doesn't show the basic sharing and caring skills a woman expected, she may still stay, hoping that his new behavior is a temporary, undiagnosed problem – and that the initial loving behavior, the 'good part', will return.

But, if a woman should talk too much about the problems in her relationship, some of her friends may start saying, 'Why do you stay? Aren't you being masochistic?' Or if a woman, on some particularly unhappy day should tell someone, 'My personal life is in turmoil,' she is likely to be met with the attitude, spoken or unspoken, 'Can't she get it together? What is the matter with her?'

Calling women 'masochists' is another example of the way in which women are made into scapegoats in relationships and are blamed for everything that goes wrong. We are challenging this mis-labelling here. What really happens in relationships that become unhappy is that they change: in the beginning the relationship usually *is* happy, but as the stereotypes we saw in Chapter 1 gradually creep in and the women tries to fight against them, the situation starts to deteriorate. Even faced with problems, most women try to stay and try to make the relationship work. But all too often their reward for this loyalty is to be labelled a 'masochist'. Surely if women left at the first sign of trouble, they would be called selfish and callous? Are women in a no-win situation?

The point is that in many problematic relationships, there are also some very good parts: sometimes a woman loves a man who is not able or doesn't want to sustain a lasting day-to-day working relationship, but the relationship or her feelings about him are still deeply moving and important to her. After all, love is not just a knee-jerk response to someone who is 'nice' to us!

Is 'happiness' always the goal in a relationship?

As one woman explains, for her the 'good stuff' is the feeling she has for her partner, not something she 'gets' out of the relationship:

> He's the one I want to love. Some other men might be easier, or more talkative, but I don't *love* them. I love him for the unique person he is – I love a person, not a relationship. I'm not looking for a person to give me the best relationship there is, I'm looking for a person I feel connected to.

A relationship can be very unstable, or even unhappy, and still provide a kind of nourishment for the soul. Somehow it opens up doors in your mind that didn't exist before.

Sometimes women say that the love they feel gives them more pleasure, more of a feeling of being themselves and being alive, even in a rough relationship, than they might find in a more 'stable' or 'pleasant' relationship:

> I don't look at my relationship as a source of happiness. I am the source of my own happiness. I look to my relationship for giving me what it gives me, not giving me a particular thing that I'm supposed to *require*. I love him because of who he is, what he is,

what we are together. Sometimes it is 'happy', sometimes it is not. I choose to stay because I feel a deep sense of connection with him, and feel fulfilled at least 75 per cent of the time. That is enough for me.

If it has no future, is it a waste of time?

Some women say that they are having love affairs which, even though they are obviously not going to last, are very meaningful to them. A love affair that is not stable is not necessarily a failure if it gives you something you need, as long as it is not destructive.

There is no shame in finding ourselves in imperfect, flawed relationships. If we give all of ourselves, our love, our allegiance, and then are 'betrayed', or if the person we love changes, this does not mean we should not have given ourselves in the first place. We have not made a mistake because we loved. The beauty of loving, of having loved, is part of 'the good stuff.'

How happy is a 'normal' relationship

Exactly how much of what you want from a relationship should you be getting? How 'good' does 'good' have to be? How imperfect is awful? And when does imperfect become insufferable?

It was years before I could appreciate my own relationship without all the tapes playing in my head about us not being married, me making more money than he did, we didn't have children, and on and on. I thought I wasn't really 'grown up', this relationship didn't measure up somehow. But good grief! It makes me happy! Why do I have to live somebody else's idea of my life?

If you are getting 70 per cent of what you want, is this OK? Is 80 per cent OK? To the outside world? To you?

Perhaps you would rather be on your own if you cannot have 100 per cent of the good stuff. Or if you cannot have a relationship in which you never hear condescending remarks, never have to witness him acting as though he is superior to you, and in which you don't have to waste energy trying to get him to talk, really talk and listen. You could be making the right choice. It all depends on *your* life and *your* needs.

NOT BEING ABLE TO TALK ABOUT THE BAD STUFF

Most women say that, although they can usually talk in general to one or two best friends, it's really hard to tell people about the frightening emotional times in their relationship:

> I didn't tell my sister what happened because I knew she would say, 'Why don't you leave if he did that?' And she wouldn't remember all the things he really gave me.

We can be in very good relationships but still find that somehow we have to hide the bad times (especially the worst times) from friends and family because otherwise they will chide us and look down on us for staying in that relationship.

Many women say they don't like others to know about the fights in their relationships for these reasons:

> He is very passionate, and when we fight he raises his voice and stomps around the apartment. I sort of like this quality, his 'Italian papa' traits, I call them. But my two friends who live downstairs have decided that I am in a shitty relationship, and they look shocked when they see us cuddling and cooing an hour later. Why can't they just see that the fights are the best way we have, so far, of working through things? And what has it got to do with them, anyway? Why do they have to be so judgemental? So 'superior'?

> Our fights are really wearing me down. We quarrel almost every night, and in the morning I go to work

feeling lousy. I talked to my girlfriends about the problems when I first got involved with him, but now I'm too embarrassed: they would just wonder why I stay.

We only saw his friends, and when I would try to talk to them about the fighting, they would sort of defend him and say, 'You can't keep nagging him or he will leave,' or, 'Don't take it so seriously,' – as if I deserved the treatment! It made me feel even worse, so I stopped talking about it.

Why is it that all too often we can't tell anybody about the really bad things that happen in our relationships? That we feel we will lose our friends' respect if they know just how terrible or humiliating something was?

Why can't others accept that just because you had a bad time yesterday, it doesn't mean your overall relationship is bad? There is no shame in having problems.

Is it embarrassing because, if a man disrespects a woman, it is like a social slur, a symbol of women's 'powerlessness' and inequality?

The first point to make is that compromising over some things in some ways doesn't mean you don't know your own mind or why you are doing whatever you are doing. Accepting some bad parts of a relationship may be your way of getting some good things, or a temporary way of exploring certain feelings you have, aspects of another person that you want to know more about.

The second point is to realize that our society has a damaging and overly black and white standard for relationships. If women are constantly being told that they are 'masochists' to stay in a not-so-perfect relationship, it stands to reason that they are going to stop talking to their friends about their problems. This fear of being labelled a 'masochist', plus feelings of loyalty to a person one loves, make women keep quiet just at the time they need their friends most.

This is the tragedy of the situation: if you can't really talk to your friends about what is going on, it makes it harder to think through your problems and resolve them, harder to separate the 'bad' and the 'good', enjoy the good and change the bad, or decide to leave or change the terms of the relationship.

ENFORCED ISOLATION IN A RELATIONSHIP

One woman describes how the spiral of not talking to friends leads to isolation:

> I didn't tell anyone for ages that I felt angry and resentful a lot of the time. I just kept it bottled up because I wanted people to think we had a good relationship, that I'd got it all together, was on top of it all. The only trouble was I felt really isolated and alone.

When you can't tell your friends what's really bad in your relationship (it may be a small percentage of what goes on, but nevertheless awful), you lose contact with them. You have to lie to them and can't be really honest and comfortable. As this is not likely to help you deal with your relationship either, the whole situation can gradually deteriorate.

Often, women find that they are loneliest when they are in a bad relationship – much lonelier than when they were 'single'. They can't talk to their partner, but neither can they talk to their friends. It is no wonder that so many women see psychologists and take enormous quantities of tranquilizers during such times.

One woman has found a way to avoid this:

> I have these old friends from college. Once a month or so, we get together and really slag off our husbands and boyfriends. It works like a charm. And it's safe: it's just us, nothing we say ever leaves the room. And nobody expects anyone to say the same thing next time or 'explain' anything. I can't describe it. It's heaven.

124

Usually, if you tell a friend, 'Last night he . . . ' and then the next day you enthuse over how much you are looking forward to seeing him, the friend will look at you with some desire for an explanation, or embarrassment, unless you explain how you resolved the situation last night. We should start realizing that a friend should feel free to discuss problems with us, and this does not mean that we should judge her, or question the reasons she has for staying with someone who 'did something like that'. We should be able to discuss the problems in each other's relationships without being told we are being 'disloyal' to our partners and without the implied question: 'If you don't like it, why don't you leave him?' How else can we understand the problems and try to work out the solutions?

Finally, remember! While you're feeling worried and guilty about a compromise you have just made in your relationship, your friends may be feeling similarly worried that *you* wouldn't approve of some of the things going on in *their* relationships! They may be feeling guilty too. If we could only talk to each other without the fear that we're unacceptable, we would feel less isolated, more sure of ourselves, and give each other more emotional support – plus, have fun talking about things. The dynamic of labelling women 'masochists' is a part of the damaging emotional contract we need to change. Silence among women, because of fear and intimidation, is another mechanism by which society alienates women from each other, dividing (and conquering) them.

IF YOU SATISFY YOUR *OWN* NEEDS, DO YOU FEEL GUILTY?

Do you have a vague, nagging feeling that you should be doing more for him, that you should love him more, find more things to do to make him happy, or look for ways to make the relationship closer? Quite a few women say they somehow feel guilty if they simply take the relationship and enjoy it on their own terms. They feel they are 'using' it:

He makes dinner for me almost every night. I come home from work, and he's already there, making it. He has done all the shopping – everything. This is really nice, although there are a lot of other things wrong with the relationship. I can't tell if he really likes doing this, or if this is his way of trying to make up for some of the bad stuff – which he won't talk about directly. I don't know whether to relax and enjoy it, or whether I should be getting out of the relationship – or if one day he's going to turn to me and tell me how unfair I am, how I'm exploiting him through his doing all the cooking!

At home or at his place, I go around in sloppy old clothes, sometimes in curlers. I work and don't talk much, I am not very sociable. Then when I go out with our friends, I turn on the charm. I wear all my make-up and everything. I like going around the house with no perfume, no make-up, but I worry I'm not keeping up my end of the relationship. Shouldn't I make more of an effort to look civilized? Try harder to be sexy?

Another woman worries that she likes her relationship for the 'wrong' reason, that: it's not what relationships are supposed to be about; it is not 'emotionally developed':

I am a playwright, and for me, the biggest thrill is when he walks in with me before a performance. We are all dressed up and I feel really elegant. He is wearing his navy suit and looks so impressive, plus it's good to know there is somebody behind me, rooting for me. But we don't have a deep relationship, he's not someone I fell head over heels in love with, he probably doesn't understand what I think my plays are really about. Yet he is perfect for me in many ways. He takes me home after the performance, or we go out to eat. It's a great luxury. What I worry about is that maybe it's not fair to him that I'm using him like this. He enjoys everything too, but I don't know, shouldn't I have a real relationship with somebody? Do I like him too much for his appearance? Is this all right?

Or sometimes women feel guilty for enjoying things they're not supposed to enjoy:

> I feel that in some deep way he will take care of me. This is probably very unliberated and very bad – I know I should be more self-sufficient – but I like him to take care of me. I like it when he pays for my dinner in a restaurant. It's terrible, I know.

> The other day we had a picnic. We went up into the hills, and he grabbed me and fucked me right there! I loved it! I loved feeling totally in his power. What my friends would say, I hate to think!

> A grown-up woman isn't supposed to like being chucked under the chin, or called 'baby'. But I feel so feminine and adored when he does these things. Am I retarded?

Are you taking advantage of him if you go around in curlers; if you are not sexy every evening; if you enjoy his macho moments in bed? Of course not!

WHAT IS A 'GOOD' RELATIONSHIP?

Of course, there are many kinds of good relationships, not just one standard model that everybody must match up to. And the kind you want at one period in your life may not be at all the kind you want later.

Here are several types of relationship; which appeals to you for your life now?

> We decided to live together about a year ago. The basis of our relationship is that we care deeply about each other and show it in small ways, like daily companionship, saving money to buy something we want for our home, giving the other a backrub when they are really tired, cooking for each other – the basic pleasures! I like the security of knowing he is there for me.

My boyfriend is a pilot. We see each other for a long weekend once a month. I was married once before – the 'standard type' – and I didn't like it. I need some space. I sure have it here! Now, I can be independent, yet fulfilled emotionally. My life has balance.

We go out about once a week. It's great. We go to parties, usually, where we have a lot of friends. We belong to a dancing society, so usually there is a lot of wild dancing and music – Latin, jazz, MTV. It's a ball to get dressed up and *go*. I look forward to it all week.

Really loving is an earthy thing. It's putting up with dirty clothes on the floor, cleaning up the bathroom after he's been sick in there, coming back when you're still really mad at him, sitting by his side night after night as he watches TV programs you hate. This love we have is gentle and quiet and unassuming. It's security and stability. It's constant and supportive. It's forgiving.

Which of these relationships would you choose? Maybe you have a different notion of your ideal relationship. Maybe you've decided that you don't want a relationship at all. What matters is what *you* want. It is *your* choice.

Here are some questions to ask yourself about your relationship to help you to see if it is 'good' and 'happy' in your terms:

- Are you 'in love' now? How can you tell?

- Do you like being in this relationship? Is it a condition of learning, enlightenment? Are there painful ups and downs, but are they fulfilling? Is there joy? Ambivalence? How important is it?

- What is the most important part of your relationship? Is it love, passion, sex, money, daily companionship, or the permanence of a long-term relationship? What is the *real* reason you want it?

- Are you 'happy' with the relationship? Inspired? Can you imagine spending the rest of your life in it? What would you like to change?

- Is the love you are giving and receiving the kind you want? Have you seen another type in a friend's relationship, in a book or a film that you would find more thrilling?

- Do you feel guilty enjoying a relationship that is not seen by your family, friends and people in general as 'right' or 'happy', although you think it is worthwhile?

- Do you want permanence in the relationship – whether or not you have it? Do you feel guilty about wanting/not wanting permanence?

- Do you feel guilty about liking parts of the relationship that you know might be considered 'unliberated'? What are they? Him talking baby talk to you? Having unusual sexual fantasies? Getting dressed up and acting 'feminine'? Letting him take care of the finances?

- How do you feel about finances? Who is making the most money? Paying the most for things? How do you feel about it?

HOW TO PIG OUT ON YOUR RELATIONSHIP!

Now, if you have answered all of these questions and you are sure what you have is on the high side of the worth-having scale, why wait? Pig out! We give you total permission! In fact, we insist!

Here's how some women told us they do just that:

On Fridays after work we go and buy our favorite snacks, rush home, put our pyjamas on, grab the cats, the dog, and my son (he's three) and we all watch cartoons and then old movies in bed. We stay there all evening. My son makes up stories and tells them to us. We just revel in our closeness, in what we have together. I look over at this man and I think, 'If I spent every Friday night like this for the rest of my life, it wouldn't be too many.'

My favorite time is when we lie in bed together and talk, late at night. We tell each other anything that's on our minds – silly jokes, deep ideas, things we're upset

129

about – or we listen to music. We make love about three days a week. Other nights it's just playing around (sometimes one of us jerks off while the other utters encouraging words), then drifting off to sleep – it's great.

I found this book of love poetry, a kind of anthology. Neither of us know much about literature, but reading these to each other has become a special treat.

Last night he read me parts of *The Prophet* by Kalil Ghibran, and some Shakespearean sonnets. We lit candles and took them into our bedroom (just a bed and walls, no room for anything else, but we love it!). It was so quiet, so peaceful. We made slow love afterwards and I had that feeling deep inside me of belonging, of being home.

He talks very tenderly to me at first. *Then* – we peel off each other's clothes and rub our bodies together. I feel so aroused when we do this. Then he'll start telling me some really sexy exotic fantasy he has about me and what we are doing, as he puts his finger just at the opening of my vagina, or on my clitoris, to tease me, make me hunger for more. I get really excited, and sometimes I masturbate myself during all this. Then, when I can't stand it anymore, I climb on top of him and he bangs into me – which I love – until he comes in one shuddering massive convulsion. Then he falls back, telling me how he loves me.

We have a lot of shared interests, and our most fun days are when we do them together: go out for the afternoon, snoop around antique shops, find little things we want to buy, eat ice-cream (that we shouldn't), go to a movie later. Then go home and have dinner, or visit friends. It's the best feeling in the world to spend a day with the man you love, and share all those things – then go to sleep later, knowing you have enjoyed it all together.

I like that he always tells me I am beautiful and that he loves me. He makes me feel I am the centre of his universe. I like that he desires me and always gets turned on around me. I like his body and the way he is, his personality and his soul, the expressions on his face and the gestures of his hands. When he takes me in his arms, well, I forget everything but his smell, his sounds, the warmth of our bodies.

With all the magazines out there warning you that you are probably neurotic for being in a 'less-than-perfect' relationship, we hope you will now have a more realistic view of the whole picture. It is important to know that even if your relationship isn't perfect, there is no need to feel guilty for taking great pleasure in the things you *do* get out of it. Certainly there are gradations and not every relationship is worth staying in. But don't feel guilty if you think yours is. Remember, it is your opinion that counts.

It is a wonderful thing to find a relationship that works for you. It is apparent that this is not something that happens every day. If you are in a relationship that is fulfilling you, good for you! Enjoy!

—6—

How to be single and love it (when all around are panicking)

Being single is the greatest. I can do anything I want
I'm free! I have more energy because I am not caught
up in learning about and negotiating with another
person full-time. I putter around the house, read
books, go to movies, eat in restaurants, dance and
travel, see my friends. Being single is loads of fun!

I love my life! How funny, I never said that when I was
in my last relationship – I always said, 'I love *him*.' But
now I can honestly say that my life has never before
been so fulfilling. People wonder why I am not
attached, why some 'lucky guy' hasn't 'grabbed' me.
This makes me want to laugh. What an antiquated way
of thinking! *I* feel the lucky person; I have *myself*!

MOST WOMEN LOVE BEING SINGLE

Most single women who have never married say that, no
matter what the problems, they love their freedom and
independence, the fun of meeting and knowing different
people, and being able to call their lives their own:

I love doing what I want, when I want – whatever that
means! Like lying around, looking like hell and reading
a trashy novel, or dressing up my sexiest garb and
dancing my head off at a club.

Travelling on my own is one of my favorite things. I love the feeling of not being tied down by another person, being the only one responsible for myself. Not reporting to anyone. If I meet someone I want to share all this with, OK. But right now this is the way I like it.

It's great to design your own life. To flirt with anyone you want, bring them home if you want – or not if you don't! To have your home just the way you want it, with no one to argue with about housework, no one else's taste to consider.

Many women, particularly those who were in unsatisfying long-term relationships before, revel in their freedom:

No matter how bad a day is now, it's 100 per cent better than when I was in my relationship!

If I want to cook dinner at seven or nine, or not at all, then I can. If I don't do the laundry for two weeks, I am the only one to complain, if I want to read in bed half the night, I can. And if on Saturday I look like a witch, and don't get dressed all day, it's my choice. I like being responsible for myself and knowing that I can make it on my own, that I am the only one I have to depend on. The disadvantages are not having that someone special who understands me and loves me, not being able to give all the love I have. But my sex life is great. I have three or four men whom I see occasionally and I thoroughly enjoy it.

I'm open for a love relationship to happen but it's just not that important to me right now. My own self, work and friends are numero uno. I love being single. I'm celibate. I don't seem to find it necessary to be involved. Independence! I'm free! I love going alone to parties, restaurants, shopping, movies. Sometimes I feel like going with others, so I go with friends, but sometimes I just need to be alone, and since this is something I didn't have in my marriage, I'm still relishing it. Sometimes others try to make me feel as if there is something terribly wrong with me for being alone, but it's their problem.

MOST WOMEN ARE SINGLE HALF THEIR LIVES!

What about the idea that all 'grown-up women' are married? Aren't Real Women married with children?

If you count the number of years (after age eighteen) before a woman is married, then add in the years after a possible divorce or between marriages (a 50 per cent divorce rate is standard in urban areas), and the number of years a woman may be a widow (since women usually live much longer than men), you will find that the average woman is single for *half* of her adult life. In other words being single is 'normal'!

Women often choose to be single

Women are less and less afraid to be single. The vast majority of divorces are now initiated by women. Even though women are quite aware that their standard of living will deteriorate when they divorce, especially if they have children, more and more they choose to be single.

If so many relationships have the built-in problems and prejudices women have described in this book, isn't it logical that many today prefer to be on their own – 'single'? Many are putting off marriage: in Great Britain, 65 per cent of women under the age of twenty-nine are single, according to 1988 government data.

It does seem that with the information that so many marriages are not happy (to wit, the 50 per cent divorce rate) plus the large number of people seeking couples counseling – as well as women's testimony here and elsewhere about their problems with men in relationships – it would be reasonable to expect that women would like being single and that this would be accepted as a perfectly respectable lifestyle. But no: a woman is *still* expected to be in a relationship if she is to have validity. Ironically, the atmosphere still prevails that there is something wrong with a woman if she is not married, or at least, in a stable relationship.

'What's a nice girl like you doing without a man?'

Sometimes I think even if I were a new Mozart, it wouldn't be enough. All my friends and family would still be saying, 'And when are you getting married? Are you seeing anybody?'

Although most women say they like being single, many do feel that the pressure 'out there' to *not* be single, to be 'looking for a man', can be a big hassle:

I get so sick of people saying that they wish I would find some nice young man and settle down. I don't want to, it's as simple as that. I wonder if they are ever going to stop saying this!

It's as if everyone thinks of you as a reject, defective – as though they think, 'If someone hasn't married her yet, there must be something wrong with her!

I just hope that some day my family and friends will believe I mean it when I say I am happy without a committed relationship. I know it's hard for them, they want to see me happy, but why can't they believe that I *am*? I resent their insinuation that I am a poor little wretch who has to put up her Christmas lights alone and has no one to share her TV dinners with. I hardly have any time alone as it is! I'm always with people. If they don't stop hassling me, I just don't want to keep up my relationships with them.

Why all the prejudice against single women? Isn't it OK to be alone, to like it? Do you *have* to be in a relationship or to be looking for one to be 'normal'? If you decide that you dislike relationships, will the world think you are weird'?

1980s media images of single women

Single women in the 80's were depicted as unstable, both sexually and emotionally – the film *Fatal Attraction* was a good example. Also, single women were often portrayed on television as angry and 'embittered', often untrustworthy, and probably neurotic and 'needy'. Study after study has shown that it is single women who are happier, married women who feel more dissatisfied. So why all of this negativity?

Of course, in the 1970s the media stereotyped women differently: then, married women were supposed to be the 'dull', 'stupid' ones while single women were supposedly 'free' and 'hip'. Now, with AIDS and the conservative mood in many Western countries, the images have been reversed: single women are seen as not fulfilling their 'natural' role, and we are endlessly bombarded with magazine articles about women who 'gave up' their careers – in fact, couldn't *wait* to give them up – for the fun and glorious experience of having babies. (It is supposedly impossible to have both.) This has happened at least once before: after World War II there was a massive media campaign to get women to return to the home and let men have the jobs. However, statistically, the number of women working outside the home has increased steadily throughout the twentieth century, until today the great majority of women, married and single, are employed.

The stereotyping of single women by the media in the 1980s reached a giant crescendo in the headline on the cover of *Newsweek*; if a woman was not married by the age of thrity-five, she had almost no chance of *ever* being married! (Oh-horror!) Especially if she was well-educated! In fact, the media reported, a single woman over thrity-five had more chance of being killed by a terrorist than of getting married!

Here is an example of the media trying to create lifestyles. An ad for a new woman's magazine reinforced this by calling its potential readers 'the new traditionalists' – showing a woman dressed (impeccably) in a suit, with a child (also impeccably dressed) beside her. With this ad, the media told us that now our place was both at work (the suit), but also more importantly with our children. Thus, we learn that we are perfectly suited for middle-management and service jobs, and therefore should not expect higher pay, 'of course' we do not want to take our jobs too seriously!

However, demographic changes mean there will be more need than ever for women in the workforce. Will we therefore see a switch in policy, with the 'working woman' – even the single woman – being more glorified?

One thing is certain: with or without media nagging, women are making their own choices, and those choices include being single for more and more years of their adult lives.

WHAT ARE SINGLE WOMEN'S LIVES *REALLY* LIKE?

According to women, being single is nothing like the media stereotypes. While women may love men, they also love the way they can live on their own. They love to run their own lives, have the luxury of paying full attention to their jobs, have time for their friends, children, and not least, for themselves. They enjoy being able to think freely without having to explain anything, being able to create their own lives.

As one woman puts it, 'There is joy in commitment to a relationship that works; but there is also great joy in a committed relationship with *yourself*.'

One woman describes her typical day:

I feel so happy this way, I want to shout it from the rooftops, 'I'm free, I'm free!' Free to run my life the way I want, do what I want. I love my friends, my work, my home. My adorable cat, Belinda. I am happy!

One thing that really bugs me is seeing pity in people's eyes when I tell them I live alone and do things on my own. They are obviously thinking that this is very sad, that I probably have some weird hang-ups. 'You're so pretty, you ought to have a beau?' and so on. They must fantasize that I spend the most horrible, desolate evenings crying in my bed because I'm alone, scanning the personals and going out on unsuccessful blind dates.

The most ridiculous part of people pitying me for being alone is that I hardly *spend* any time alone! In fact, I see more people as a 'single' woman than I ever did when I was in relationships. My life is far from lonely, in fact it seems saturated with humanity.

My typical day is so full I can hardly keep it straight: At 7.00 in the morning I get up, shower, play with my cat, meditate, dress, make a call to a friend or my Mum. At 8.30 I either have a breakfast meeting or go to my favourite café where I have met the most fascinating woman; she is the assistant to a philanthropist and she tells me wonderful stories of their travels. I get to my office at 9.00 sharp. I really love my work, I'm in advertising and I'm good at it. I get paid very well. I like most of the people I work with, and usually go home at the end of the day feeling quite satisfied. At 12.00 I have a lunch break – I go to a café or to the park, usually with a good friend, a different one every day. We talk and laugh and rehash the previous evening's events in both our lives. I try to leave the office at about 5.30 to go to the gym where my trainer really works me hard. I work out, take a steam bath, where I usually see my friend Pam, shower, and go home. Evenings go something like this:

By 6.30 I am home in my little flat which I love. It has all *my* things in it, it is totally me. I listen to my answering machine and return some calls, and then get dressed for the evening. My best friend usually comes over for tea, but if she is going out too, we talk on the phone while we are both dressing. At 7.30 either I go out with a date, or I meet friends and we go to the movies, out to dinner, go dancing, or some other fun thing. Sometimes I go to a spiritual workshop I have joined. I try to be home by 11.00 and I cuddle with my cat after a long, luxurious bubble bath (with more talking on phone!). I get into my glorious bed and read

a good novel or watch the TV. Sometimes a friend
comes home with me and watches with me. Lights go
out at around 12.30 and I say my prayers, grateful for
another full day and drift off into a deep sleep.
   I don't know about you, but I think my life is terrific!'

Despite the stereotype of the single woman as basically
unfulfilled and 'neurotic', most single women's lives are
spent working, seeing friends, taking care of family – not
pining away in some lonely corner in a rumpled dressing
gown, watching soaps or mooning over their favorite rock
idol.

But wouldn't you *rather* be married?

What does being 'alone' really mean? Interestingly, more
women say they feel lonely inside a non-loving relationship
than they do being 'single'. The main reason for this is that
it is much more isolating and terrifying to be with someone
you cannot reach than to be on your own, enjoying your life
and your friends.
   Over and over again, women say that they have many
good women friends, sometimes friends of a lifetime, and
that their communication with them is the closest of all their
relationships. So it is not surprising that single women feel
less lonely. They have more time to be with their women
friends because their time and energy is not consumed in a
relationship; they have more chance of feeling 'heard' and
'seen' on a daily basis:

   I think I had a kind of constant, low-grade depression
   when I was with him. But it wasn't till I was out of the
   relationship that I realized it. He used to shut me out,
   close himself off. I *was* alone, even though we were
   together. In my life now, I have great friendships
   where I am never shut out. I haven't felt loneliness at
   all, now that I am single.

   I'd say one of the greatest gifts of living on my own has
   been discovering the depth and quality of my friendships. I hadn't had enough time for them before, as I

139

had always been so wrapped up in my marriage. Now I have friendships which fulfill me far more than the relationship ever did, and I can really be there for my friends. It's a whole new way of life I'm discovering.

SOCIAL HASSLES YOU KNOW AND LOVE

Fighting the stereotypes is no picnic

Remember those times when you are expected to be 'in a couple', 'escorted' or 'attached'? In these situations, women say, while *they* are perfectly content being on their own, others project feelings of nervousness and condescension on to the 'single woman' – as if they don't really believe she is single by choice. What is she doing there, anyway? Somehow her situation is embarrassing and they think she is probably out to 'get her hands' on every guy in the place.

As one woman points out, the assumption is not only that women should be married, but also that if they are not, they are probably trying to 'trap' men into it:

> I still don't understand why everyone always thinks women are trying to get some guy to marry them. People seem to think that any woman who is unmarried is dying to get hitched. They never say that about men, at least I've never heard it. And even if she did want to get married, what would be so bad about that? It's as though the most disgusting and undesirable thing in the world for a woman is to want to get married, and the most appealing thing in the world for a man is to avoid it!

'Desperate predators out to get their man!'

In this social atmosphere single women are all too often seen as some kind of desperate predators, who can't be trusted. One women tells a story about coming face to face with the assumption that she couldn't possibly be out alone by choice:

140

I was sitting in bed the other afternoon after a luxurious nap, the sun was streaming in the window. I felt so good – I had cleaned my flat, been to an art gallery with a friend, and spent all afternoon reading the paper. Now I had an overwhelming urge for Indian food. I *had* to have it . . . there was nothing for it but to take myself to my favorite Indian restaurant, enjoy the food and read a good book.

When I got there, the guy who is usually at the door greeted me and said, 'I can't understand why such a lovely girl is eating alone this evening.' It doesn't bother me with him, because he is nice and really doesn't understand that this is OK with me. Anyway, it wasn't condescending. But what really annoyed me was this guy who was sitting alone, staring at me. I made it quite clear to him that I didn't want to be stared at and was enjoying my own company. You know, there are definitely ways you can show this while not being rude. Most sensitive people with manners would pick up on it.

Well, not this fella. First he sent a waiter over with a drink. I told the waiter to thank the gentleman, but I was 'enjoying a dinner alone and don't drink'. When the waiter went over to him to say that, he started laughing! The wanker obviously thought there was no way that I was telling the truth, that I must be playing hard to get, because the only reasons a woman ever goes to a restaurant alone are 1) she can't find anyone to take her, or 2) she wants to get picked up/laid/paid for/meet her future husband.

I went to the loo, and when I returned, he was sitting at my table! I asked what he was doing there. He laughed again, and said the classic, 'What are you doing going out alone? Some poor bastard really blew it by leaving *you* in the lurch on a beautiful evening like this!' (all said whilst looking at my chest and legs).

By this time I was so sick of the whole thing, I just asked him to leave. He got all put out about it, saying, 'God, what's the matter? A guy tries to talk to you when you come to a restaurant alone, what do you expect? You shouldn't go out alone in that case! Jesus!'

It was the same old thing again. I go into situations where I am perfectly happy, in fact I don't even think about the fact that I am alone and that it may be weird to some people, and I meet with the same attitudes. It is never acceptable to most people that you are alone because you *want* to be. That is the last reason they ever think of. I have a great life, but people seem to want to take it away from me. They *want* to think that I'm lonely and depressed. Reality doesn't get through to them!

These kinds of hassles, as another woman describes, often result in women having the feeling that they shouldn't go out alone, they ought to stay at home or be with a man:

An old friend was getting married and had invited me to the wedding. It was a special invitation for me, because we had known each other so long and had fallen out at one point.

It never occurred to me that I would take anyone. I was going to see a lot of friends there, and I didn't want to ask anyone to go with me, I wanted to be free to speak with whoever I wanted and to leave when I wanted to.

After the ceremony, everyone went to the reception in a beautiful old building. I got myself a drink at the bar. I noticed that all the other people at the bar were men – as if women can't get their own drinks. I felt odd, feeling they thought it was a shame I didn't have someone to wait on me too! When I started to talk to people, every single one asked me who I came with! When I said, 'No one, I came by myself,' one of the women actually frowned and touched my arm and said, in this sort of baby voice, 'Oh, you poor thing! We've got to hook you up with somebody.' It was so uncomfortable. I finally left thinking I was an alien or something. After a while you start to question your-self, too!

142

Most women have been in situations like these where they are 'expected' to be 'in a couple' and are looked down upon if they are not:

> Even my women friends are amazed when they meet a woman who is attractive but unattached. If she doesn't have a boyfriend they think she is 1) consumed by her work, 2) emotionally imbalanced, or 3) gay! Why can't the first idea that pops into their heads be that she is enjoying life by herself?

Men with commitmentphobia:
convincing him you don't want to get married

Many single women say that all the talk in the media about 'husband-hungry single women' is having a bad effect on the way men relate to them: many men are assuming that *all* single women are 'guilty' of this 'obsession'.

Women are finding it very hard to fight this prejudice which invalidates their every action. No matter what she says or does, the man reacts as if she is 'guilty' of 'trying to get him', as this woman found:

> Men I know make jokes all the time about the girls they meet, only now the jokes are different. They used to laugh about how women always wanted to stop them from having fun, and about women being clingy. Now they joke about the fact that girls they meet at bars and parties are only looking for a husband. I think all the attention the media and books have given to the eternal quest for marriage on the part of single women has hurt us greatly. We already had a hard enough time convincing men that not all of us were trying to trap them into marriage, and therefore couldn't be trusted – we were just 'conniving bitches'. Now every inch we had gained has been totally blown. We are having to start from scratch.

Another woman describes what happened on a first date she had recently:

143

I met a man at my new job who was very attractive, well-dressed, and sexy. He was also very attentive and listened to everything I had to say with what I thought was interest and sincerity. There seemed to be a lot of potential for us to really enjoy each other.

I was really nervous getting ready for our first date. I hadn't dated in quite a while, no one interested me enough. But this guy was different. I found myself thinking about what it would be like to go to bed with him. Exciting!

When he picked me up, he looked adorable. I could feel his excitement, too, and he even told me how he had not looked forward to a date this much in a long time.

We went to a movie, had a long dinner, chatted and laughed and told each other our life stories. I was enjoying him, and it felt very natural and good.

When we got home to my place, I asked him up for a nightcap. During our conversation, he asked me what I was doing over the weekend. I told him I was going to a friend's wedding. I then commented on how many people were getting married, and how weird it felt to me. I asked him if he found the same to be true with his friends, and if he felt odd still being unmarried.

Well, I actually saw him blanch! Almost as if he had a physical reaction to my question. From then on the conversation deteriorated because he assumed, from that innocent question, that I was yet another woman 'out to bag him'.

I was incredulous. He sat there and went into a diatribe about how much he resented women he dated who were basically out to get a husband (*him*) and were 'just pretending to be independent'. He said it drove him nuts to sit and listen to women yak about how much they loved their careers over dinner, when he *knew* all they really wanted was to get hitched and dump the career as soon as possible! He said he felt like prey and was sick of it.

My first reaction was to tell him that I could understand why he would feel like that if some women were obviously only interested in his earning capacity and whether his family had a lot of money. I told him some similar experiences I had had where the first thing a man asked me was whether I liked children, etc. I was trying to empathize with him. I couldn't believe that this guy would keep on pigeon-holeing me and *all* single women.

But he didn't even listen to my side of things from that moment on. Finally, I explicitly told him that I was not at all interested in marriage at the moment, I even said the words: 'I don't want to get married.' How much clearer can you be? And I felt demeaned, even saying it. But if he needed to hear it, I thought, well . . . but he just withdrew emotionally from the moment the subject came up, and saw me as some kind of desperate, wimpy enemy. I was so disappointed. We muttered 'goodnight' and he left.

Here is another woman's reaction to the ridiculous prejudices against single women:

I walk by bookshops and see all these books on 'How to find a husband in thirty days' and 'Getting him to the altar' and I get really pissed off. If *I* see those books, then men must see those books, too. Not to mention all the television shows with audience participation that harp on about this. Now, when I meet men, they are all wearing this invisible sign which reads, 'Don't even *think* of mentioning marriage in my vicinity.' It is so arrogant. It makes me want to say, the minute I meet one of them, 'Hi, I'm Julie, and I don't want to get married!'

This is yet another example of the social pressures that contrive to put women on the defensive. And women often remark that all this pressure becomes stronger around the age of thirty.

Thirty and not married: the terror?

Interestingly, just at the time when many women begin to consider whether they would like to try marriage and a family because they've reached an age when biologically they should make a decision, they are faced with additional pressure. They can't relax and decide: they are under the gun to decide. How many of us have been asked, 'So when are you going to settle down and have children?' as soon as someone – even a comparative stranger – discovers that we're thirty?

We then start to worry about the stereotypes being hurled at us:

> All of a sudden I woke up and realized most of my friends are married and then, gee, is there something wrong with me, am I going to be single for ever? I'm starting to think I'm going to be, starting to cope with that. You wonder what's going to happen when you're older and that kind of stuff. It's a little scary, but I don't really think I'm ever going to get married. And that's dumb because that's like saying, well, can't you take care of yourself?

> The pressure to get married or find a life partner is great now, mostly internal. I feel that if I don't become involved soon there is something wrong with me. But I don't want to make a big deal about it, or I'll feel like a 'typical' picture of a desperate female trying to drag some poor unsuspecting male up the aisle.

Many single women say they are so assaulted by the assumption that they are desperate to get married that it becomes a real task to maintain their own independent perspective, and not let all this pressure interfere with their enjoyment of living on their own.

One way to defend yourself against this barrage of irrational pressures is to listen to the women, here and all around us, talking about what their lives are *really* like.

THE DEBATE OVER WHETHER TO MARRY

It can be very difficult to think clearly about whether we want to be married or to live life on our own, surrounded by such strong social pressure.

The majority of single women have mixed feelings about marriage, questioning their own feelings and motivations:

> The idea of a family and love and holidays together sounds just great and I've been waiting so long, I would like to try it. But what if I don't like marriage? Will I be able to get rid of him? Or will he hurt me? I never wanted to marry someone if I didn't really love them, if I wasn't in love – other men who wanted to marry me, I just didn't want to be that intimate with – so here I am. Maybe I just think now I should get married because 'everyone else is doing it'. But the word 'married' to me sounds synonymous with being adored, being accepted. I guess I would love to be able to say, 'I'm married'.

> I'm in a state of confusion now. I've been involved with different men often enough to realize that I could never have been happy married to any of them. But I feel the need to have a permanent man. Do I really need it or is it just something we women have been reared to believe – that we need to have a man to make our lives complete?

Some say they are just not interested in marriage. They never want to get married, at least not in the foreseeable future:

> Marriage seems overrated – people reaching for a type of security that just doesn't exist anymore. It is based on assumptions that aren't realistic. As a contract, it's very unfair and inequitable. I hope I never get married.

> The idea of marriage scares me right now. I think it is important for some individuals, but not all. I do not think I am monogamous by nature!

Even when they are in relationships they like, some women still do not want to get married:

> We are compatible on all levels – we laugh, we cry, we share many things, the same activities, and we are

147

politically alike – conservative. I can tell my lover
anything, and usually do! I am extremely happy,
and so is he. But as to the future – we are too young
to be looking for a lifetime commitment.

Sometimes these women feel guilty for not wanting the
permanence of marriage:

I love my boyfriend, but I don't want to plan my life
with him. I've been seeing him for about a year, and
I get sick of all the questions about when we are
going to move in together, etc. Why can't I just like
it the way it is? Am I shallow?

Women who have been married before are often particularly reluctant to remarry:

As I sit here writing this I feel like I could go on for
ages, write a novel, about the bliss of being on my
own. It sounds overly dramatic to say that I experience my new single status as if I had been let out of
prison, but it isn't, I really feel that way. I feel like I
spent eight years denying who I was, living with
daily disappointments, denied anger, put-downs
and judgements – like I was living in a country
where those were the rules. Now I live in another
country, one filled with my own choices, my own
feelings, one where who I am is celebrated – by me,
and my friends. I never again want to live the way I
did when I was 'attached'. I couldn't have felt less
attached!

I had been married for most of my adult life, and am
now forty-eight and divorced. It is great to run my
own life and not answer to anyone but myself – I
love that. But I don't love being considered 'incom-
plete', 'unloved' by so many people. I am fine! Why
can't I be seen as what I really am (living on my own
and satisfied with that) instead of people trying to
insist I must be unhappy, lonely and a 'loser'?

148

Still other women, especially some who have never been married, do want the commitment of marriage:

> Intellectually, I realise that people can be single all their lives. I have some role models (women) who were single, and so I feel that I would have some support for a decision that I might remain single. However, emotionally, I seem conditioned towards marriage. Some part of me does not want to be single forever.

A lot of women say they feel embarrassed to 'admit' they want marriage (no wonder, with women chided for being 'desperate'):

> It's hard to admit I really want a man, I really want a marriage. No matter what I know politically, no matter how impossible or stupid it seems . . . I still want it. But I feel a great deal of pressure not to be preoccupied with love or romantic feelings, not to get carried away by a love affair.

Some women decide they would like to try marriage after experiencing a series of unsatisfying relationships:

> I want to marry because I don't want to split my love up. I have been in love in the past, and later we fell out of love, and then I went through that whole cycle again, and I don't want to anymore. I want to marry a man I fall in love with, and give him my love and be faithful to him and only him. This would be very satisfying to me.

> It's been fun. All through college I knew a lot of men. Some I loved, some were real terrors. What I really want now is my own gem, and I want him for a long time. I want to have fun at Easter and know at Christmas we can remember Easter. I want to plan a dinner party and know Ed won't have changed to John after I've told all my friends who's coming. And, most of all, I want to really love someone.

But understandably, after what we've heard women say in this book, a lot of single women are wondering if a committed relationship will ever work out for them:

> I don't know, I seem to meet guys who I get involved with but it never lasts – for one reason or another. Usually it's because they want me to be someone I am not, or it is just 'not right' between us. Sometimes I think I had better bring my expectations down a peg or two, or I will be alone forever – never meet anyone. I like my life now, but I would like to have a lasting relationship in my future. But I'm wondering if it will ever happen to me.

> Either I want something lasting and they don't, or they want something lasting and I don't. It never seems to mesh. I'm beginning to think it never will, and this scares me.

The fear that nothing will ever come of their relationships bothers many women; but these women are not 'husband hunters' – they simply want to develop deeper relationships.

Should I marry the 'wrong guy', or risk staying single for ever?

What *if* you don't meet 'the right man', or someone you really feel good with, someone who is a true addition to your life? As one woman says,

> I married to get everybody off my back. I was thirty and I just couldn't deal with it any more.

With all the pressures we have mentioned, it is not surprising that some women question whether they should 'settle' and just marry 'somone nice':

> I keep thinking – if I don't marry this one, I may never marry anyone else. Maybe he's the best I can find.

All these pressures ... He's such a nice guy, but, I don't know, there's a lack of enthusiasm I feel, maybe he has a lack of enthusiasm about life, maybe I want too much, maybe I'm a romantic junkie at heart, waiting for Prince Charming or something like that. But why do I have to marry someone I'm not crazy about? On the other hand, I may never find anyone else. Will I be sorry later?

FEARS ABOUT REMAINING SINGLE

What if I wake up one day and want a baby, and it's too late?

Most women, at some time in their lives, think about whether they want to have a baby. While many women are quite happy to choose to live their lives child-free, there is always the possibility, many fear, (while their famous 'biological clock' is madly ticking away) that they will suddenly wake up one day with a deep, undeniable longing for a child:

I have always been pretty sure I didn't want a baby, but lately I've been wondering if some day I will want one, and there will be no one to make one with! Plus, I don't know if I could financially manage to have one alone.

I'm twenty-eight, and have never really thought too much about having a child, except to think of how agonizingly painful it would be! But lately I've had these romantic fantasies about being in the delivery room with an adoring husband holding my hand throughout the whole thing. It seems like it would be the most profound experience. I still think I don't want one, but if I'm going to change my mind I should do it before too long.

I get this tug deep in my belly when I am around babies. Is that weird? I don't tell anyone about this, though – in my circle, it wouldn't be considered very chic.

151

'If I live on my own for ever, will I be able to afford it?'

Another fear concerns money. Many single women, though enjoying their independence, wonder if they will be able to support themselves all their lives. This is not surprising, since many factors make it difficult for women to earn a good wage all their lives, and most women are not taught about life insurance, investments, or general financial strategies. However, the fact is, we are doing remarkably well. The highest success rate for new businesses in the United States is held by women who start their own businesses; and, of course, it is the women in most families who do the monthly accounting and keep the budget.

Still, having to carry the financial weight of living on their own indefinitely is especially hard for divorced single women with children:

> I love having no one else to answer to financially, but I get worried about money, too. I watch my married friends and how much more they have (materially). I mean, what if I was ill? There would be no money coming in and I would lose my lease and my car very quickly. If I was married, my husband could carry the weight for a while. Or, even if I was in a relationship, at least someone could buy me groceries and stuff. I feel guilty for feeling like this, but it is true.

> I am currently four months pregnant and working for a large corporation. My boyfriend and I plan to get married as soon as we find a flat, but I'm beginning to wonder if that will ever happen. I sometimes think maybe I'll be bringing up this child alone. I'm frightened. What will happen then? I don't think I can make it.

If you're living on your own now and coping, there is a great chance you will still be able to do this in twenty, thirty or forty years time. And of course even if you *do* start living with someone, this is no guarantee of permanence or income – for either of you.

The unmentionable fear: getting old

Many younger single women worry, 'If I don't get married, won't I wind up alone? Nobody will want me. I'll be old and ugly!' This is the fear that is fed to us day and night: you won't be able to 'get a man' especially after forty!

The result is that many women think 'I've got to keep trying to meet someone, or maybe just grab the next guy that comes along and settle down before it's too late!'

How many of us are haunted by the image of a 'feeble little old lady' at her door, 'pathetically' waiting for the milkman, because he is the only person she gets to talk to every day? This is nothing to do with the reality of choosing never to marry, or not to remarry. It is a fantasy encouraged by people who think old is 'bad' (and that female 'old' is even worse).

Such fears are not based on the *reality* of older women's lives, but they can be very paowerful.

> I don't think so much about falling in love right now. I'm too busy! What I am afraid of is growing old alone. Being a dependent old lady. The kind of person everyone has to worry about because she's alone. Pathetic. It's hard to imagine, because my life is so full now. But if I were married, I would have children and grandchildren – I would not end up alone.

It is quite understandable to be frightened and uncertain about facing the future on your own, however sure you are at the moment that this is what you want. Everyone, at some time or another, has doubts about the choices they make. But listen to these examples of women in their sixties and seventies who are living on their own and loving their freedom. Theirs are inspiring lives and an example to us all!

OLDER WOMEN – HAVING A BALL!

The pervasive view that older single women are 'unhappy' is not based on older women's own accounts of how they feel:

The word single really irritates me. It sounds so negative! As though I must be miserable and depressed.
Pitiable somehow! But I love my life – and everything
in it. I've been in relationships before, I was married,
but now I choose to be on my own. No one ever seems
to view being on your own as a choice. But it is – my
life is full and really exciting. I love every minute of it!

A lot of single women over sixty-five would rate their lives
high up on the 'happiness scale'. Listen to this charming
seventy-year-old:

I am a seventy year old grandma who lives alone, and
is very alive. I have two dogs. Love to study and love
kids, especially my grandchildren. Right now I'm
happy. Tomorrow, who knows?

My lover died this spring. I miss him. But in a way, I
am relieved! I don't miss the put-downs. Since he
died, I pass the time reading dime novels. My goals?
To write a little, fish, to design. Face death with
humor!

Right now I'm enjoying being single. Usually everyone else – when I'm not single – is more important
than I am. Now I'm important and enjoying it! I always
looked for love till now. Now all I've got is me, but I
don't mind, I like it. Being single, you can do what you
want. Don't have to do anything.

I admire women who can get up and go. Sally
Shelton, Gloria Steinen, Eleanor Roosevelt, Indira
Gandhi, Margaret Thatcher, Margaret Mead, Jackie
Onassis, Elizabeth Cady Stanton. I believe in the
women's movement. I'm a feminist. It made me
realize what I'd missed. Although I'm a nurse, I
should have been a lawyer.

I enjoy looking glamorous. Femininity means being
sexually pleasing to men, yet firm in one's own ideas. I
still shudder at masculine women. I enjoy beautiful
clothing – although I live in jeans on a farm. I feed the
horses, but can look well when dressed. I don't wear
makeup (like Ma). Half the time I look a sight, so I'm

not very feminine. Have fun though. If you ask me how I look at seventy, I'd say – truthfully – awful!

To women today I say: Love your kids and encourage them. Then do your own thing. With regard to love, don't worry about happy endings, life doesn't have them! But you can enjoy it meanwhile.

Some older single women certainly dispel myths that they are at home knitting and their sex drive has long since 'dried up':

I am sixty-five years old, have four grown children. I share my love with a seventy-two year old man who wants to marry me when I am through with my divorce (my second marriage, thirty-eight years).

Sex with my lover is enjoyable. Usually he stimulates me by hand to orgasm. When we are not together I masturbate. I orgasm easiest through masturbation, but if I do not catch one very soon, I give up and let go without. But most of the time it works.

Thus the stereotype of being 'old and alone' is basically inaccurate: most single women over sixty-five like their lives very much. They enjoy their friends, their work, gardens, lovers, – all facets of life. While lack of money can be a definite problem, happiness is a different matter: many women say they feel *happier* when 'old and alone' – happier than they ever have been.

TRANSITION

It can be hard – or at least feel unusual – to start a life on your own after not being single for a while:

It has been so long since I was 'available' that I sort of don't know what to do. A lot of the rules have changed. Apart from a killer disease out there, I also hear all this banter about the New Man and the 'sensitive guy' – but that's really a load of crap, from what I see. I mean, it just looks like a new way for them to get what they want. They still win in the end, they score big.

But for some women the transition is easy:

I'm divorced after twenty-eight years of marriage and I love it. I am still OK looking, and right now I have two lovers. Believe it or not, I am a grandmother, too! I have one six year old granddaughter and one two year old grandson. My kids are a little surprised that I have such an active sexlife, but they're getting used to it! Ralph (my main man) cooked the turkey last Thanksgiving, and it was the first time in at least twenty years that I heard laughter at that table. My marriage was based on 'the less said, the better'. Now I have two men who talk and laugh with me, even in bed. I finally have asked for what I like in bed and I am getting it! I have never felt better!

One woman describes how she has begun to see herself and her relationships with her friends, in a whole new way:

Being single has been very good for me, but it has been hard, especially at first. I was so used to being in a loveless marriage where neither of us was satisfied, but it was financially secure and fitted in with all the social 'shoulds' of being a couple, both working, both successful, etc. I had been with him since grad school, so had not really lived on my own in the 'real world'. When I decided to leave, after a lot of agonizing, I found a little apartment nearby where some friends had flats in the building. They helped me move my furniture, paint the apartment . . .

At first, it was very hard for me to adjust to being in my own apartment. I was still grieving over the relationship, and all my possessions reminded me of 'us' and 'the way it used to be'. I didn't know how to plan my social life so that I would have things to do in the evenings. All my evenings had been spent with him, and all our socializing had been with mostly his friends. I didn't know how to let it be known that I was a free agent and was ready to have a full life filled with activity of my own. I didn't know how to go about that.

The first few months were hard. It was summer, and really hot. I took a risk and went in on a house at the beach with seven other people I didn't know. Every weekend I would go out there, and it opened up a whole new social life for me. I also invited friends from the city out there, and soon my datebook was crammed.

I had a fling with a doctor at this time, which was really fun because it reawakened my sexual drive which had been dormant. I was so turned off emotionally at home that I had become turned off physically. He was a great lover, and I couldn't get enough! But he got serious very fast, and I didn't want that, I wanted to keep my life unbounded. I had a feeling I would be glad about it later.

Well, I am. My life today is completely different. Gone are the endless nights of fighting or silence, of trying and failing to make anything work. Drinking and smoking too much because I didn't know what else to do.

Life can be great, if you choose to do what is best for you. Being single is, so far, my favorite way of living.

The struggle for autonomy: designing your own life

One woman in her late twenties describes how she has convinced herself that her own experience is more valid than any predetermined, predefined life-style:

I started relationships when I was fourteen and have been in them until last year when I turned twenty-eight. They've never lasted more than about a year, and they always overlapped. Most of the guys wanted a girl on their arm to squire around, to make them feel like a king. I guess I was looking for a sort of identity – though it took me a few years to figure this meant that I was not worthy enough on my own, that I only really

157

existed in society's eyes (and my own) if I had a boyfriend. It was odd, because I was well-educated and knew about feminist issues, but for some reason I never applied them to myself.

Well, once I did, it was like a volcano exploding. It was a revelation. *I did not need to be attached to a man to be a full person!* I made a commitment to myself: I would stay out of relationships for a year until I could be clear about what I wanted in a relationship, or whether I wanted one at all. I would develop my life and fill it with all the things I love, and nothing that I did not. I would not compromise. I would not spend time with people I didn't like, or do things I didn't want to do (except go to work on some mornings when I would rather sleep!) I took up riding again, I read a lot more. I worked on being much healthier physically.

Well, one year has turned into two, and today I can hardly remember myself before: a person who was not true to herself, trapped somehow. Loneliness was a feeling I used to have when I was in those lousy relationships, but I'm virtually never lonely today. I spend a lot of time with great friends. I go out on dates and have sex once in a while.

Sometimes I worry about being alone for ever, but then I realise that this is just my old way of thinking. If my life continued this way indefinitely, that would be fine with me!

Today, most women – while they may love men – also love the way they can live on their own. They love the way they can run their lives, pay attention to their jobs, their friends, themselves, the way they can think freely without explaining anything – how they can create their own lives!

OUR FUTURE, OURSELVES

In praise of solitude

So far, we have seen that being single does not necessarily mean you are alone; in fact many women find in some ways they are *more* connected to others and to the world, when living on their own. But supposing being single means you are often alone? Is that bad? What is the great fear that seems to surround the word 'alone'?

In relationships or not, most women love to spend time alone, have the luxury of time for themselves. When asked, 'What do you most like to do for yourself?', most women chose activities that were done alone, such as taking a bath, reading a book, going for a long walk, sitting down and having a cup of tea, or almost anything solo. Why?

This brings up a very profound point: given the enormous social pressures on us to express only limited parts of ourselves with others, it isn't surprising that women love their moments of solitude. Many women say that they can be more themselves when they are alone than at any other time. They say being alone is not 'sad' or 'bad', but very refreshing and restoring to the spirit. Time spent on their own, they say, allows feelings to come to the surface which are unclear, and enables a recentering process to take place. It also allows time for creativity and planning, dreaming for the future. And what will that future be?

There are two futures we speak of here: your own personal future, and our shared future as women – the future of our society, our world.

What this woman says is true both for her personally, and for us all as women:

Being single is a time I take quantum leaps in self development. It seems to release a surge of creative energy in me. I think I am a better person for the time I spend alone.

Perhaps it truly *is* a new time in history for women: if we can ignore and get beyond the heavy social pressures on us (and if our financial situation is not too difficult), then for the first time we can make our lives anything we want.

Finally, one woman in her fifties describes memorably her experience of being single, how she has re-created her entire life and who she is today:

I was a wife and mother for twenty-five years, my work was basically homemaking. My greatest achievement is my four years of college. I didn't graduate, but I still see it as my greatest achievement, beyond mothering . . . beyond anything else. I don't feel I was in the world or in any way in charge of my own life until I got divorced.

The approximate total income of my household is about $5,000. The best job I could get when I left the marriage was as a cleaning woman – that's my experience, what I did for twenty-five years. It's worth it to be on my own. Being in control of my life. Absolute independence. I love doing what I want to do, being with who I want to be with, staying out as late as I want, changing my mind if I want, living the way I want, listening to the music I want.

I could never really communicate with my husband, never share with him. The divorce was like death and rebirth. I felt relieved that I could start living again. I still feel relief nine years later.

What is my sex life like? Sometimes there is no sex life. But I enjoy periods of no sex as well as sex or being sexual by myself. I relate more aggressively the older I get. I used to be strictly heterosexual, now I get a great deal of pleasure making love to women occasionally too. My most important relationship with a woman has been my relationship with my daughter. She is my best friend. She is a ray of light in my life. I love her dearly.

To women I say – you can be who you want to be. Look how I've changed! I've revised, I'm like T. S. Eliot. There will be time for a hundred more revisions. Oh, a thousand revisions.

What more could we possibly add? She has said it all. There will be time for revisions for a thousand revisions for all of us. The 1990s will be a decade of change for women. Once we have begun to rely on our own experience, this will release a surge of energy and ideas for the reorganization of society. Join in! We need you!

160

Women as Friends, Women as Lovers

We have been talking almost exclusively about relationships with men in this book, because we are trying to unravel probels of the heterosexual emotional conract to make way for a new type of life for ourselves in the 1990s. But a large component of our private lives is our relationship with other women – whether as friends or as lovers. What are relationships between women like?

Most women describe their friendships with other women as very happy, very important to them. Women rely on each other, being alternately children, mothers, sisters and friends for one another – sometimes all on the same day! There are moments of letdown, of course, and even betrayal, but these tend to be the exception, not the rule.

WOMEN LOVE THEIR WOMEN FRIENDS

When asked, 'Who is your best friend? What do you think of her? How do you feel when you are together?', women often describe relationships full of beauty, strength, learning and powerful emotional attachment:

> I have a sense of owning the world when we are together, a feeling of oneness: not in a romantic sense, but I feel anchored to the planet. Anything is possible with our friendship backing me up! I also find her hilariously funny. That usually results in a lighthearted

161

feeling when I leave her. Most of all, I feel I am OK, that all is well. Nurtured.

I always feel great after I see her. We talk about everything that's going on in our lives. It seems that she is the only person with whom I can talk about absolutely anything. She makes me feel better than anyone. If I could only have a relationship with a man that even came close to our friendship, I would be totally happy!

We have been friends for thirteen years. She's smart, she knows me like a book, I can never fool her. She makes me aware of things about myself I don't even realize, she makes me think but won't solve my problems for me. When we are together we talk for hours. I feel like there is a strong bond between us.

One woman, in loving detail, draws a portrait of her best friend:

Jen is my oldest and dearest friend. She has style, and most people think she is adorable to look at. She is sexy, funny, and very bright. We have been through a lifetime together. Sometimes I marvel at the length of time we have known each other, and also at the amount that has happened in both of our lives, together and apart. I marvel at the peaks and valleys of our friendship, although the valleys were never that low, only little 'glitches' caused, primarily, by distance. But we have always come together again, and I have never wavered from undying loyalty and true respect.

We met when we were thirteen, at school. I don't remember our first meeting, but by the time half the year was over, we were fast friends, spending the night at each other's homes and swooning over our favorite pin-ups. We were from different backgrounds, but cut from the same cloth. We would spend hours in hysterics over something funny one of us said, a funny thought or comment.

The first party I ever went to where there were boys, Jen was with me. We look a lot of time (weeks) deciding what to wear, and she spent a whole afternoon taking the rhinestones off a shirt I wanted to wear that night, just because I didn't like the rhinestones. I remember to this day how much that little thing meant to me.

As we got older, we started to hang out as a group, she with her boyfriend, me with mine – the boyfriends were best friends, so we were together all the time, which was great because that is what we wanted anyway! We both were already aware of the injustices one suffered as a woman, being defined by men as sexual toys, then being put down for the same definition. We were always battling against that. But we had fun anyway, partied together, went through pain over men together, shared our deepest secrets and truths with each other. We were inseparable.

When I went away to college, she and I had some problems at first. My whole life changed, I adopted a new vocabulary, new attitudes, made new kinds of friends. I can imagine how threatening it was for her to receive letters from someone who said she was me, but who sounded totally different! But when I went home at Christmas, we talked it out. One thing I really love about Jen is she never hesitates to speak her mind. I have never been as good at that, but the amount of it that I do, I owe to her – she showed me. She has a very strong character, and I love her for it.

Since then we have lived in two different countries. I think about her on almost a daily basis. Our friendship has now lasted for seventeen years. It is hard to describe how I feel about her, beyond the story I have just told. Her courage, discipline, sense of abandon, sense of humor, loyalty, ability to love, sense of her own high self-worth, her triumphs over family, work and relationship problems, her ability to see the best side of a situation, her help in guiding me when I don't know which way to turn, her undying tribute to me by calling me her best friend – all of these things are why I

love her. I would love her even if she behaved like a
total jerk. It is a non-refundable love, an acceptance of
her as a friend for life.

Most women speak very enthusiastically about their
women friends, describing a special connection they only
rarely find with men – a high level of understanding, great
verbal communication, and a deep caring and loyalty that
survives changes and upheavals: distance, breakups,
deaths. Although these intense relationships sometimes go
through difficulties, they are relatively infrequent and can
usually be overcome.

Emotional closeness

So often women say they wish they could communicate
with the men in their lives the way they communicate with
their friends; women seem to 'know' them, without agonizing over difficult and ambiguous communication and
emotional barriers:

> When I really need to talk on an emotional level, really
> let someone into my heart, it's always easier and more
> rewarding with my best friend. My boyfriend doesn't
> seem to like to talk like this, it makes him uncomfort-
> able. I like to know I can laugh, cry or whatever, and
> that anything I say is acceptable. I wish I could have
> this with him.

> I can talk to her about anything. There's no ego and
> false pride involved like there is with most of the men I
> know. I hardly ever feel satisfied after a conversation
> with a man the way I do when I've talked to her, or to
> any woman, actually.

> Men tend to reduce the world and all its parts to
> mechanical pieces. They don't see life as a whole.
> Women have more of an overview, see things as they
> relate to each other, not in isolated bits. I go to women
> when I need advice, even women I don't know really
> well. Once when I had a big decision to make about a

relationship and my best friend was away, I just blurted out all these feelings to a woman I'd just met. She was so calm and so interested. She didn't try to *tell* me what to do, she just listened. Her genuine concern and empathy really came through and supported me, it helped me trust myself.

Women say that their conversations with other women are more detailed, more involved in searching out, listening for and hearing the other's inner thoughts, working together to explore the feelings one person is trying to express. They lament the fact that men often seem to work against them in this endeavor, leaving women feeling they are swimming upstream. One woman analyzes it like this:

Men I have loved seem so closed compared to women I have known. It seems as though guys have such a hard time with being open – I suppose they're just more cut off from their feelings. They think demonstrating such a range of feelings is 'soft' or 'weak'. It's hard to relate to a person like that.

On the whole, women do not end up feeling drained in their friendships with women, in the way they often do with men, because the emotional support is mutual: neither is giving but not receiving understanding and love.

Is it harder for most women to talk to a male lover because there is more vulnerability between lovers than friends? Or is it easier to talk to women because they are less competitive, have a different style of relating, and prefer to be supportive? While it is true that love relationships can be more intense and demanding than friendships, most men also say that the people they feel are the easiest to talk to are their women friends or their wives. Since both women and men find it easier and more pleasurable to talk to women, it is clear that the way women communicate is preferable – the loving and nurturing way.

165

WOMEN'S WAY OF RELATING: THE FOUR GIFTS

What are the skills that both women and men find so attractive? Women say that their friendships with other women are open and spontaneous, that it is easy to talk, that their women friends are good at listening and giving feedback, rarely judgemental – and rarely pressure them to conform to any pre-defined pattern or put them down if they do not do so.

Emotional support, no questions asked

One of the greatest gifts women give each other is the knowledge that they are there for each other as emotional supports, and that no judgements will be made. This level of acceptance is the foundation of many friendships: it creates a feeling of safety that makes it possible to be open and to express oneself freely.

Women usually say they can speak more freely and honestly with each other than with men, who may refuse to talk, or even trash them for what they are saying:

> I know that I can tell her anything, and she will never react by saying, 'God, I can't believe you *said* that, how can you *feel* such a thing? That's horrible!' I've had many men saying that to me.

> My sister and I can talk about anything, no matter how intimate or shocking. That's because she always listens and she never judges me – she only offers loving support.

> No matter how long its been since I've seen my woman friends, we click and can talk about anything. They're non-judgemental, supportive, and I know if I need them they'll be there. My secrets are safe with them and they'll be honest with me.

> I'll never forget the first time I opened myself up to this older woman who is very close to me. It was at the beginning of our friendship, which has grown into one

166

where she is my emotional mentor. I told her some deep, dark secrets about myself, things that I had never told anyone. I was shaking, but I had a feeling that she would be able to understand me. When I said each thing, I checked her face and she didn't look shocked at all. All she said was, 'I'm so glad you told me that, that you feel safe enough with me to share this way. It means a lot to me.' I couldn't believe that she was thanking *me* for such a valuable gift *she* had given. This acceptance of me changed my life, my relating to others.

Listening – with genuine interest!

Often women enthusiastically praise the way their friends show interest in hearing their thoughts and experiences:

When I talk with my women friends, I know they are really listening and concentrating on what I have to say, whether it is an important thing or a little thing. It spoils me, though, for in the outside world men don't listen the same way, and I am always surprised (one more time) when they don't. Why can't their talking be this respectful?

When we talk, she really is interested in what I say. What I think about things, what I do with my day, people I meet, they are all interesting to her. She is curious about all the things I do, and her interest is respectful, exciting, loving – I know she wants the best for me. She helps me when I am making a decision, and gives me such a feeling of validity, as if everything I do in my life is important.

My friend is beautiful and talented, although she probably wouldn't admit it. She has done some amazing things with her life, has come a long way from when I first met her. I was her support in the beginning of our friendship, but it has turned into a two-way street. Now, when I am feeling bad, I can call her and she will completely identify with whatever it is I am going through, even if she hasn't gone through it herself. She has an incredible ability to empathize. It means so much to me. When I call her, at home or at work, I always get off the phone feeling warmer, more supported, more strong. I love her very much.

Constructive criticism and ideas

Women say that the kind of support they receive from their women friends often results in enlightenment or learning. Their friends may tell them when they've made a mistake, help them to overcome destructive habits, or remove themselves from situations that they might not see are bad for them. Yet this advice is easy to take because it so clearly comes with a sense of love and loyalty:

At first, her constant comments about the relationship I was in annoyed me. She was always saying that I deserved something more and that I didn't need to put up with this any longer. She was right. But I resented it, I thought she was criticizing me. I didn't see that it hurt her to see me in so much pain. The time had long passed where I was getting enough from this man to make it worth staying – I wasn't. Finally, I started to notice that, although she criticized him for hurting me and criticized me, albeit gently, for staying with him, she never told me I was unacceptable. In fact, she said that she identified with me and had been where I was once before. When I realized this, I valued her even more. Her advice was sound. She was right.

Another woman describes how her best friend has always been there for her, giving criticism and love:

We have been close friends for about two and a half years. There are a lot of things about us that are the same, and a lot of things that are different. From the beginning, we have shared everything on a very deep emotional level. First it was just talking, now it means

168

pouring out our hearts to each other, letting each other see our vulnerabilities and our tears.

I went through a devastating relationship about two years ago, and she was there for me every step of the way. When she thought I was being self-destructive, she told me so and helped me discover new ways of 'being'. When I needed nurturing, she was there with lots of it. We lived around the corner from each other, and I spent nearly all my waking hours with her, sometimes talking, sometimes just eating and watching the TV in the quiet. Because of her constancy and support, I was able to go through that experience. I am a better person for it, and a better person for sharing friendship with her. Now, we live in different cities, but I still feel as close, and we are still there for each other, we call each other for reassurance and love when we need it. She will be my maid of honor when I marry this summer. I can't describe what this relationship means to me. It means closeness and intimacy, support and strength. It means everything.

Courage in times of trouble

How often have women been each other's support in times of difficulty? In the nineteenth century and earlier, women generally were the ones who helped each other during childbirth, acting as midwives or doing whatever was necessary. When women need a helping hand, a baby-sitter, someone to lean on, a place to stay, more often than not it is another woman who is there.

Who would you call in a crisis? Women often know what to do:

I had a friend in college who was very attractive, very Catholic and very bright. She was popular, she worked hard and did not get caught up in as much of the wild partying as I did. When I found out I was pregnant, I was devastated. I knew what I had to do, but I didn't want to go alone. When I called her, there wasn't a

169

moment of discomfort between us. Straight away, she called the clinic, made an appointment for the next morning, then she came over, fixed dinner and spent the night with me. She never once let it show that my decision to have an abortion bothered her morally or religiously. I was so impressed by her loyalty and steadfastness and her ability to make me feel accepted for what I was doing, and for taking charge at a time when I simply couldn't. I will never forget how she helped me, and what it meant to me.

Lamentably, these four gifts of women's friendship are undervalued by society. Both women and men seek them out and enjoy them, but rather than being praised for these qualities, for their well-developed emotional literacy and ability to relate, women are labelled negatively as 'too loving', 'overly emotional' and so on. Where are the positive stereotypes of women's virtues?

Historically, many women are now trying to repress these qualities. Women are under great pressure from society – at work, for example – to be 'more like a man': 'control your feelings', don't talk 'too much', develop 'male' gestures. Other women are fighting this type of pressure, refusing to wear 'masculine' business suits if they don't want to, refusing to try to be 'one of the guys' on the job. If women who act more like men are rewarded with advancement and higher pay, who can blame women for trying to modify their behavior? And yet, won't we all be much less well off if women are no longer there with their traditional warmth and support? Isn't the answer that more men should learn to be more loving and open, less harshly competitive?

We need to change the basic value structure of society as that empathy and a desire for the common good are valued over aggression and war-like qualities. Such a change could cure many things that are wrong with our society, such as the exploitation of the environment. Men's dominating, exploitative attitude towards women is mirrored in our society's attitude towards nature; our assumption that we can use the environment for our own purposes, that we

170

don't have to interact or show mutual respect for all forms of life is what has brought us to the current impasse.

BREAKING UP WITH A FRIEND

What we have said up till now has all been positive but – surprise, surprise – friendships between women are not always perfect!

> I have found it very difficult to express any anger towards her. She is so incredibly sensitive that she breaks down in tears whenever I try to tell her she has made me angry, which I think is an important part of close friendship – the freedom to be honest with each other about your 'bad' as well as your 'good' feelings.

> There is nothing better than being with her when she is feeling good, it's the most satisfying time I spend with anyone. But she gets incredibly sad, and I have begun to feel totally frustrated by it. Nothing I say seems to help, and she doesn't come out of it very quickly. I'm just expected to go along with it and listen to her for hours and then enjoy the good times when they come.

> I am jealous of my best friend. I have never admitted it before. I feel so guilty about it. But when she spends more time with other people, I hate it and feel left out. I try *never* to let it show.

And not all problems can be solved. Some women tell sad stories of breaking up with a woman friend they loved:

> My best friend and I are kind of drifting apart right now. She wants to be a dancer and she is doing some kind of exotic dancing. Now, I've never seen her do it but I have an idea of what this is like. She is not totally nude but she doesn't wear a whole lot and she just basically dances in these bars and she gets paid pretty well for it. She likes this dancing and she knows I disapprove of it. It's really changed our relationship. I

171

find the whole thing absolutely nauseating, the fact that men just sit there and watch her, not because she has good dancing technique, but because she is using her sexuality to get their attention.

She has become involved in a job and a relationship that are interrelated (her boss is her boyfriend), and now she doesn't have time for me. I drop by their business sometimes, but she is always too busy to talk and suggests that we get together on the weekend but then she always calls it off, has something better to do. I feel I was just a stop-gap until she found what she really wanted – a man and a career. Now I'm old news. This hurts me a lot, as I came to depend on her emotionally, to need her input into my life, to express with her and to laugh with her. I feel cheated.

My 'best friend' is a beautiful, brilliant woman who has been through a great deal. She has always had this awful habit of thinking the world will wait for her. Even in the old days when we were all hanging out a lot, she would always be late for dinner parties, or sometimes call and cancel, or sometimes not call at all and not show up. Everyone would laugh (me included) and say, 'Well, ha ha, that's her, dear Anna.' We all worried about her constantly, about her health and well-being. She drank too much.

The last few years she has stood me up so much I'm beginning not to be sympathetic. I have invited her to come and stay with us for a week many times. She always says she is definitely coming, but then she never does. I hid my disappointment and hurt and carried on saying the usual, 'Ah, that's Anna.' But recently it has really started to get to me. I would never treat anyone that way.

I think the final straw came when I invited her for this New Year's Eve. I was excited she was coming because she lives so far away and we spend so little time together. I made reservations at a fabulous restaurant (at her suggestion) and went shopping for special foods for her (she is vegetarian). She called the day

172

before and said, 'Sorry, love, but I'm with friends up in the country and I can't seem to get anyone to move to travel to where you are.' She blamed it on everyone else.

When I hung up, all the disappointment of the past eighteen years welled up in me. I am in the process of writing her a letter saying that I can no longer accept my friendship on this basis.

ATTRACTION TO OTHER WOMEN

Shyness: how to handle it

Don't friendships sometimes border on being 'in love'? If we feel so enthusiastic about another woman, aren't we 'in love' a little bit? Can we tell the other person? Is it necessary? What would we say?

In general, there is no vocabulary for such feelings of attraction between women who do not want to have a lesbian relationship, but who nevertheless want to express the intensity of their friendship in some way. How do women deal with these feelings? What are the choices?

In Victorian times, women's letters and diaries show that women spoke and wrote to each other much more intimately, using such phrases as, 'my dearest one', 'when I am with you, my heart sings', or, remembering their time together, 'your warmth was everywhere'. These are not unusual phrases; they were commonplace and appear over and over again in women's documents of the period. Also, it was quite customary for women to walk in the street together arm in arm, or hand in hand. This was not considered in any way 'strange' or unusual, just a sign of friendship. Today this heritage lingers in the customary kiss on the cheek women are 'allowed' to give each other on arriving and departing (as long as they take care to keep their bodies in an A-frame position, so that areas below the neck never meet!).

How did our physicality become so strait-jacketed that now anyone we touch for more than a minute must be a 'lover'? That the only sustained physical warmth we can get is from someone we have 'sex' with? The line between polite treatment of a friend and physical intimacy has become too hard and fast.

Why is it that with a friend we have known and loved for ten years or more we 'cannot' sit cuddled up together watching television? While this might just be possible while we are still in school, it becomes less and less 'acceptable' as we get older. Married women in particular are supposed to become the 'property' of the man in the marriage; remnants of this idea are to be found in the feeling, discussed in Chapter 5, that we cannot talk about the deeper parts of what goes on in a relationship with our friends, or this would show a lack of 'loyalty'.

There is certainly nothing wrong with using words we normally reserve for a lover in speaking to a friend, if this is how we feel. Physical warmth and intimacy between friends should be possible, not every physical gesture should be seen as some 'preliminary' to sex. But who will be the first to initiate such brave gestures?

When friendship becomes sexual

One woman tells how, while in a difficult heterosexual relationship, she found herself gradually falling in love with a woman friend:

> The best relationship I have ever had was with a woman. A friendship that developed quickly evolved, slowly, into intimacy. I was living with an intolerable man at the time, someone who would play cruel games with me and even hurt me physically. It was a tumultuous five years, filled with jealousy and distrust.
>
> I met her at work. It was instant 'like' – not physical, but a connection we couldn't deny. Gradually, I found myself wanting to be with her more than I wanted to be with him. I felt warm, valued and safe with her; with him I only felt hollow and a deep sense of lack. Everything I wanted in a relationship I was receiving from her: nurturing, respect, validation and trust. He was stifling and suffocating, she delighted in my self-

expansion. For the first time in my life, I was free to be
me.

Within a year, it just happened . . . that first kiss. I
don't know if it was the secrecy of it, or the excitement
of doing something that is viewed as 'wrong', but it
was so full of feeling . . . I was exhilarated. It felt so
natural. There was no shame. It was new for both of
us, but it felt so right. Eventually, I left him and moved
in with her.

Another woman, who has had relationships with a man
and several women, describes why she prefers relationships with women. The differences she finds in communication and level of intensity are the reasons she gave:

The conversations with Anne-Marie would be so complete and involved. For instance, 'Oh, this dinner
we're going to, I have really mixed feelings about it.
How do you feel about it?' And then we would
speculate on our thoughts, talk about it. Or if we were
having a fight, one of us might say, 'You're really
taking advantage of me,' and then the other would say,
'Tell me why – explain to me how you feel about that –
tell me what you mean, in depth.' Then she would
listen to me for five or ten minutes. She might complain about what I said, but still she would listen.
That's the relationship I had with her.

With a woman in a relationship, nothing's taken for
granted, whereas men sometimes have the attitude:
we'll just cruise along here, and everything will be OK.
With women, there's always a discussion, always, and
the direction of the relationship is constantly up for
revision. At least, it's like that with us. Whereas in an
argument or a discussion with my ex-boyfriend, I
would get – nothing. It would just be totally disregarded. Or if I pushed, he would say, 'You're crazy, I
just refuse to discuss this.' And that would be the end
of the conversation. I would rant and rave, on and on,
without him listening, without him paying a bit of
attention to me – he would usually start doing some-

175

thing else at the same time, like cleaning his desk. And then after I had done ranting and raving, he would say, 'See what I mean? You're a complete lunatic.' And he'd walk away and not say anything else.

I definitely get more response from my woman lover. Talking with her is completely different. (Of course, it depends on how patient we are that day with each other.) But more often than not, when I bring up something, or drop a remark, the response I get is, 'What do you mean? How can you say that?' or, 'Tell me more about what you meant by that.'

On the other hand, sometimes with my previous woman lover it all became such a complex psychological interaction, it became top-heavy. Anything you do you know can be interpreted in thousands of ways by the other person, and to discuss it becomes this massive thing. During one of these discussions, in fact, my previous girlfriend just told me to fuck off. She just couldn't deal with so much analyzing of feelings, there was too much intensity and focus on the relationship for her.

Of course, it's true, to a degree, when you have two women who are telling each other all their inner thoughts, both very intense, it can get really turned inward – but still, it's great. I think that your identity develops through these discussions. It's a real process of discovery for me – both of me and of her. It's a great experience.

LOVING ANOTHER WOMAN

Of course, love between women involves many of the same human problems women face in heterosexual relationships, but there is still a feeling that love between women *is* simpler and *does* work better – and for many it is more serious, on a different plane:

Falling in love is not as important as not falling out of love. These relationships I share with women with whom I am for ever in love – with or, probably, without sex – are the relationships I value above all others. The lovers who are closer than friends; friends deeper and more multifaceted than lovers. The ones I will always meet up with again, and know they are somewhere out there in the world, not forgetting our love, using it to strengthen them.

I believe a love relationship between two women is far more serious than one between a man and a woman. Women run on a higher emotional level than men will let themselves, and they get to deeper levels with each other.

Is love between women more equal? Seeing what other women have said here about the differences in style between communicating with women and with men, it would seem that the answer is yes – these relationships are more equal, and conducted in a different way.

Gay women's descriptions of their lives with their lovers are often filled with warmth and jubilance, when they tell about the kinds of things they like to do together:

I love being a woman and being gay. Nearly all my friends are gay women. I have a lover now, and we have an exciting although turbulent relationship. It's not all roses by any means! But it feels good and she sparks my imagination. I think I love her.

Laughing, talking, drinking, eating, discussing – we make love through all of it. We're passionate in different ways all day. It's wonderful and fun being together.

I want to do everything there is to do with her, and see all there is to see. There is nothing I do that I would not rather have her share with me than do alone. We love to go to parties together, walk in the park, play softball, take hot baths and make love. We also love reading to each other. But, mostly, I just love to wake up in the morning and look over at her and know that she loves me. It's the best!

177

One older gay woman describes how she feels about her life, and warmly describes her large circle of friends, many of whom are ex-lovers:

I'm gay, been gay all my life, have many friends and ex-lovers who are friends, and a large circle of women I am close to. I have always loved being gay. Being accepted as an equal among equals. I think women are wonderful, I just love women, I always have. Most of my life, I have been in long relationships. I went with one woman for ten years, and another for seven. Those were the longest, but it was always four years, three years – things like that. I was always going with somebody ... There was a woman I really loved – she was very, very good-looking and rich (maybe not too bright). We had a strong sexual alliance – the physical relationship was just sublime. I melted when I saw her, I forgot where I was and who I was in her arms. I floated away to some other world ...

If I could generalize in the abstract, women are more caring. Of course, I am a woman, so it's easier for me to relate to women. I think they're nicer people. Besides, I like dealing with equals, with peers. I like people who are like me ... I like the way women look and smell. And feel. They feel and smell and look better than men do. They even sound better. I like everything they do better.

I just love living. I like what I do. I like socializing. I love going to the movies. I love reading books. I love being alone. I love watching my VCR. I love going to parties. I love dancing. I love walking my dog. I love the beach. I get a lot of pleasure out of life. I just love the things I do.

Sex between women

Gay women describe very multifaceted types of sex with each other:

When we make love, both of us assume different roles all the time – during one night, we might roll around, one on top of the other at different times, one taking charge one minute, the other taking charge the next. It is sexy, but it is also a statement of the way we are together – no one is in control more than the other. We lie in each other's arms, smell each other's breath and the scent of our bodies mingls together. I feel a calm and deep passion afterwards, like I have been made whole. It is nothing like sex I ever had with men.

My sex life now is happy, joyful and fulfilling – actual sex play to orgasm happens only about once a week, but the touching, snuggling and holding is at least as important and that's every day. Sex is like dessert – a treat when we have the time or are in the mood – wonderful, but not the core of our love.

I feel desired when she makes love to me. I also feel she recognizes my vulnerability and is treating me gently.

I like rough, passionate sex because it goes beyond the barriers of 'niceness' that so many women build around themselves. There's no feeling of holding back, as there so often is with politically correct, gentle sex.

What does it mean to love another woman?

Who is to say which is more 'natural': to love the opposite sex or one's own? In ancient Greece men would have been hard-pressed to answer that!

Many women here have expressed the deepest feelings of love, joy, passion and sorrow for the women they love, either just as friends or as friends and lovers. At one level or another, all of us have the chance to share in the beauty of women, the power of womanhood.

THE PROBLEMS AND POLITICS OF WOMEN'S FRIENDSHIPS

We may love our women friends, but how seriously do we take them? Do we really think they are as important as men? As capable of filling a seat in government? Of running a major corporation? Or, even, of thinking rationally?

Although women praise their friends and obviously love
them, these friendships often exist outside the power
relationships of jobs, families, and so on. Our love for each
other is almost 'outside' society in a way, not a part of the
'real' world.

How many of us think, since men run the world and
have more money and power, that they are more important? We may not want to think like this, but on some level,
it appears that we do. One of the ways this lack of respect
for women shows is in the casual way some women will
still cancel plans with another woman if a man asks them
out.

When women put men first: cancelling appointments

Many women have felt hurt by the way their friends take
the men in their lives more seriously:

> I have been cancelled at short notice by my friends
> when a guy calls them up, maybe on the very day we
> were supposed to be going out. It really pissed me off.
> I resent being considered less important, being taken
> for granted. I would never do that to another woman.

> She always waits for me to call *her* now, and never
> makes plans for us to spend time together anymore. I
> think that once you have a guy or get married, every-
> thing is different.

> I remember once cancelling an arrangement with a
> woman because I had had yet another huge fight with
> my boyfriend and he had called and said he wanted to
> have dinner with me. She got angry and said, 'It seems
> you take your relationship with him more seriously
> than your relationship with me!' This upset me a lot,
> and I spent some time defending myself in my head
> about it. But eventually, I realized she was right. I
> think it was insulting to her, a kind of attitude I don't
> want to have. Now I think it is reprehensible to put
> men first. My women friends are very important to

me. Commitments made to them are just as significant as commitments made to my boyfriends.

Do we spend too much time talking about men?

While most women enjoy telling and hearing from their friends what is going on in their relationships with men, some think that to talk too much about men is just using each other – as if the basis of the friendship is a mutual sympathy society over men, rather than a real interest in each other:

> What I've always disliked about women friends is their constant talk about their involvements with men. It bothered me that we didn't talk enough about our *own* plans and problems.

> It has hurt me in the past when I felt my only place in her life was to talk about the men she was going out with. There ought to be more going on in a friendship than just talking about guys and what they do to you, how they make you feel.

> Probably one of the most tiring parts of my being with women friends is that so many of them are continually talking about men. I get tired of discussing whether there are any 'good men' here. There is more to single life than finding a man! I tell them, 'Who cares?'

> I've disliked women friends who constantly talked about their relationships with men; we talked about what they should have been talking to the man about.

But most women do not feel this way; most say that these conversations are extremely important because they enable them to think through how they feel about what a man is doing, to reaffirm their own value system:

> I never could have survived this relationship and left him without her constant support and always being available to listen to me crying and babbling. She was

181

solid, humorous and kind. Without her to bounce my
feelings off, I would never have got to the truer, deeper
ones, the ones that were buried for so long.

Is spending a lot of time talking about men 'using'
women friends? Or is it part of working out a philosophy of
life?

Far from being 'silly girl talk', these conversations are
extremely important. Also, they are often highly philo-
sophical: through discussing particular situations and
trying to decipher together a man's assumptions about
women and 'love' (How does he actually feel? Why does
he behave as he does?), women clarify their own feelings
about what is going on, see the situation more clearly,
and think more lucidly about what they want their
response to be. These conversations help women evolve a
sophisticated set of values, 'women's ways of being'. And
they are sharing their feelings and experiences with a
friend.

Most women say that comparing notes like this helps
them sort out whether they are getting what they really
want from a relationship, and also keeps them
emotionally afloat, avoiding the isolation that can set in
for a woman in a problematic relationship (see Chapter
5).

The situations many women discuss with each other
relate to the emotional aggression we defined in Chapter 1.
In these conversations women hear and acknowledge what
other women, their friends, are experiencing. This is
especially important because society denies that these patterns of attempted emotional and psychological domi-
nation exist. Without digging them out and looking at them
with someone else, women would have to accept what
society teaches: that if there are problems, they are the
woman's fault, she should re-adjust her view of things, or
possibly go to a psychiatrist if the problems persist. While
talking to a psychoanalyst or counselor can be helpful at
times, most professionals do not acknowledge that the
status of women, and men's assumptions about them, are
a large-scale social problem, which makes relationships

difficult. This needs to be considered when discussing what is going on. So the help women get from their friends in figuring out how to deal with various stereotypes is enormously important.

FEAR OF OTHER WOMEN

Jealousy and envy

What about the old cliché that women are really catty and jealous of each other? It is less true today? Was it ever true?

Some women can bring themselves to talk, usually guiltily, about those good old-fashioned feelings of jealousy – usually envy, or a fear of being left out:

> My friend Ellen is prettier than me. I wish that I did not feel threatened by that. I tell myself to be self-confident, I promise myself that I will applaud her for her physical beauty, but when she walks in, in a knock-out dress, all confidence and smiles, it's all over. I try to pick her apart in my mind, and can't wait to discover a flaw! It's terrible. Theoretically, I want to encourage attractive women like her to be part of our circle of friends, and to not be afraid for her to be friends with my boyfriend. Do I have to see every pretty woman as a threat? But I do! I suppose I am all for the empowerment of women – except for women who are more attractive than me! What a hypocrite I am!

> My boss is beautiful, rich and powerful. I am insanely jealous, it is just too much! I hate her, I want to *be* her. But I never let it show, because I know that would make me look a wimp. I *am* a wimp! Why can't I get over this? It makes it worse that on top of it all, I *like* her so much.

> I was on holiday in a place where there are nude beaches. I felt jealous and threatened by the women there because I was worried the man I was with would think they were sexier, and had better shapes. But had

I been alone, I probably would have still said to myself, 'Why can't I look like that?' Or, 'Why can't I be so nonchalant in the nude?' I didn't feel trust for those women, and I never tried to make friends with them. I would like myself better if they weren't such a threat to me.

One woman describes conquering these feelings of jealousy:

I used to feel very jealous of my best friend, although I hid it and covered it over. She always seemed more together, more attractive to men and more in charge of her life. I decided to tell her how I felt, hoping this might dissipate the fears. It was a risk, but I thought, 'What the hell, I can't stand feeling this way, it's too painful. What can I lose?' And I really wanted to be friends with her. When I told her, she was surprised and very warm. She told me all the things about herself that she didn't like, her looks and personality. She told me how envious she was of parts of my personality and my legs! After she let me in on her insecurities, I felt so much stronger. Since then she asks me for reassurance just as much as I ask her. Now I don't look at her in the same way.

Feeling insecure with women

Will other women criticize us, we sometimes fear, like our mothers may have done? After all, for most of us, it was our mother who had the job of supervising us, disciplining us, teaching us, and so our mother was more apt to 'criticize' us, as well as encourage us. This criticism, from one so powerful, could feel very painful, and seem to limit our ability to be free, to create our own identity.

The result is that women, like men, may have a gut fear of other women, expecting the worst, even though our relationships – expecially at work, for instance – may be good on the surface. We can be too quick too bail out when we hear any negative words from a woman, much quicker than when we hear criticism or condescension from a man.

Is it possile that we, like men, have a love/hate relationship with women? That we, like men, don't respect other women as much as we do men? And this implies, of course, that we do not respect ourselves as much, either. It is a sad state of affairs. This is something we must face and deal with; not to do so means we will be destined to repeat ourselves, we will perpetuate the same negative stereotypes about women we deplore so much when they are used against us. We ourselves will hold each other back.

If we believed in each other, we could do anything. After all, we are over 51 per cent of the population. Why can't we unite, and at least elect people who make certain women receive equal pay with men?

TORN ALLEGIANCES

The reason we don't have solidarity is not because we are 'naturally jealous', but because we don't really think highly enough of other women – yet. And we aren't even aware of this – yet.

For example, one woman, studying to be a lawyer, was heard saying, 'I don't want to be referred to as a woman lawyer when I graduate, but as a person.' It is quite understandable that she does not want to be discriminated against because she is a woman, pointed out as 'different'. On the other hand, there is something else involved here. Men do not mind being classed as 'men', in fact, being a man, a Real Man, is something most men are proud of and want very much to achieve. But for many women, who have internalized the general view of society that women are less, being classified as a woman reeks of social disapproval.

Of course, it would be ideal if society did not focus so much on gender, if we did not have this problem to deal with. But it does classify us from birth, on every form we fill in thereafter, and even in the way we are addressed: 'Mr' and 'Ms'. Since this is the reality we live with, we must, it seems, take a stand regarding our own category. Why not be proud of our identity, proud of what women have achieved? There are many books that celebrate women's past, present and future, even though women's contribution is trivialized or discounted in most history textbooks – and in many contemporary newspapers.

The situation for women is not dissimilar to that of blacks. A few years ago, blacks were seen by everyone as second-class citizens. They still receive terribly unequal pay, but due to 'black pride', a change in consciousness, they are gradually turning the world's view around.

Do we think men are more important?

This phenomenon of not really respecting ourselves or other women – even though we may love them – comes out frequently in women's statements about their mothers. The majority of women say they grew up feeling closer to their father than to their mother – that they admired him more, wanted to be more like him, not at all like their mothers:

> I identify more with my father because he has always had a job and I do too. I want to be more like him than I want to be like my mother. But my mother I can talk to in a way I never could my father. She is always there for me – not on every level, but for bottom line survival, I know she is there. She is the one I turn to when I've got to be *sure*.

This identification derives from the fact that our fathers tended to have a higher status then our mothers, were usually more important 'in the world', had more money, were more exciting, and perhaps had more time to play with us, since they were not involved in housework. But once again, what we see being internalized here is the idea that women are less – less desirable, less fun, less interesting, and so on.

This is a frequently unexamined part of our relationship with our mothers – and ourselves – although when women see their women friends behave as though men are superior, they recognize this behavior for what it is and often remark that it hurts them.

Fear of male power

Another way all of this comes out is that women frequently say they notice how much their friends diminish themselves in men's company – that they are afraid to express their thoughts or may withdraw a remark immediately if there is any sign of male disapproval – becoming true wimps, in fact!

> My friend has such strong opinions, I really love it when she gets going. But put her around a man and she becomes this demure little thing, nodding in agreement. It makes me furious.

> I admire women who can love other women and not be ingratiating with men. I hate women who have split personalities – one for their women friends and one for their men friends. I admire a woman who loves who she is and doesn't try to live up to someone else's expectations.

One woman describes how she first noticed this wimpy tendency in herself, then stopped herself from behaving in this way:

> I realized one day that I always felt denied when I had been in social situations with men, but it had always been a vague feeling. Then I realized one of the reasons was that I didn't really act like who I was with them. It's hard to explain, but somehow I knew that if I was to be who I actually am – strong, animated and argumentative – I would turn them off. And since they were 'meant' to like me, I had to tone myself down to the point where I hardly existed. When I realized this, it was a wonderful feeling – because I also realized that I was no longer going to do this, and that was fine with me. If they didn't like it, too bad.

But I was not going to be a wimp around men anymore.

Fear of speaking out

If we can't count on our friends in public, if we see them bow to 'male' power, how can we respect them? It is difficult for many women to watch their friends treat men and women differently, to trust men as if they deserve more status and respect. Or to see that, even though their friends realize the injustices they suffer from the male-dominated world, they don't take any action to challenge that 'authority'.

Women talk about seeing these dynamics work in subtle but infuriating ways, even in every-day social situations. It can be hard for us to speak out and make our thoughts known when we have always been taught that men's thoughts and ideas are more important. And if a woman *does* voice an opinion in a mixed group, she may be told she is trying to 'dominate' the situation, or the men present. But if she is silent, she can be labelled 'wimpy'. She may be reminded by the men present (or even some women) that men dislike 'aggressive' women! So what is the solution?

Obviously what *you* feel and think is as important as anything a man may feel and think. You have just as much right to say what you think as any man does, and it is at least as valuable. Of course, what stops many women is the fear of men's power. (Perhaps he is your employer?) But if we stick up for each other we can conquer that power! We must speak out without fear in all situations, overcome our intimidation and support and defend each other as we do so.

What do *you* really think of women?

Ask yourself these questions to discover how you *really* feel about the women in your life – your best friend, your sisters, your work colleagues, your mother:

● Who is your best friend? How do you feel about her? Emotionally? Politically?

188

- Do you feel guilty about things you have done to women in social or business situations? Proud?

- Do you use your friends' emotional availability and nurturing as much as men use yours?

- When was the last time you phoned your friend just to say hello and ask how she is – not to cry on her shoulder?

- Are some of your women friends 'less attractive' and less successful than you? Does it mean anything that they are or that they are not, or is it of no importance?

- Do you think women are silly because they spend so much money on make-up? Do you, and does it bother you? Or do you sometimes think it is fun to enjoy adornment?

- Do you ever walk down the street holding your friend's hand? How long can you do it before you become uncomfortable?

- Do you expect less from women than from men? More? Do you think they are more or less capable?

- Do you speak up when men are discriminating against women? Or do you usually try to avoid confrontation?

- If your best woman friend was looking for a position in government, would you secretly think she wasn't as capable as the man she's running against?

- Do you *really* believe that women should be half of the ruling body in your country/company/household? And would you like to be in that group?

- Would you feel as married if a woman performed the ceremony?

- Do you know the date for International Women's Day?

WOMEN'S SOLIDARITY: THE KEY TO THE FUTURE

If we don't take women as seriously as we take men, we will never have the solidarity to change things.

And we *do* need to change things: the highest percentage

of those living in poverty throughout the world is women and children, and this percentage is rising. A woman who divorces can expect to see her income drop sharply after the divorce; most do not receive child support. Women still earn just over half as much as men, on average, for similar work. Is this fair? Do you want to change it? Do you also want to change the emotional inequality that plagues most love relationships between women and men?

Men may have more power than we do. However, if women stick together to lobby for good basic child care, and an end to sexual discrimination in education and wages, we could change things in no time. Why is it that so many women fail to perceive or act on this? Is it because, as 'second-class citizens', some women would rather identify with men? And so feel (falsely) superior?

Only if we support one another and have courage can we make equality a reality. Without solidarity, we will have nothing except more socks to wash, more emotional unfulfillment and increasing domestic violence, whether physical or emotional. Being proud of each other is the key to improving our status – and even our relationships with men we love!

To change things, why don't we unify and work together for goals we can all agree on – such as equal pay? And meanwhile let's make changes in our personal lives – change the emotional contract we have been talking about. Insist on men changing, get them to owrk with us, lobby for equal rights with us. And always, always, whether it's in love or friendship, let's stick up for each other.

Believing in each other

What is the most important advice women can offer each other now?

My advice to women? Love and respect each other, the rest will come.

Open your eyes. Value your women friends, love yourself and each other first. Don't be afraid to be strong and define *yourself*.

When I was about 23, I finally realised how men behaved in relationships and how much energy I put into making relationships work, I somehow stopped loving men. I feel that supporting and valuing women and putting my time and energy and love into them is the best thing I can do to change the world. I am sure that this will change men too. It will force them to question their behaviour and they will start to talk to each other and give each other more emotional support. Everytime a man is left by a woman, it forces him to question his behaviour – at least a little bit.

Make sure you always have a support group of women. Women are bright and strong and emotionally expressive, loving and motivated.

If I could give any advice to other women, it would be to clear out of your life the things that make you unhappy. Don't stick with ugly jobs or ugly relationships because of some future thing you're hoping for. Don't suffer now in anticipation that it will be better in the future. Spend more time on the things that do make you happy. And love other women – don't let the system get to you! *You are great and you can make it!*

If we continue to carry in our hearts society's prejudices about women, if we don't change things, including our own attitudes, all the work women have done recently for women's rights could be washed away: equal credit ratings at banks, the right of women to be single, the right of women not to be battered in marriage. The rape of women and physical battering are outrageous, and any human should be able to see this, yet it is only within the last few years that women, demonstrating great courage and bravery in speaking out, have managed to make these seemingly 'natural' human rights important national issues.

Let's keep up the tradition. Any steps towards equal pay, for example, that we can make, which will affect you directly, will only be made by working together. Don't let us down – don't let *yourself* down! Let's do it!

Many women now *do* support each other. This does not mean that all women we know are perfect, or that we ourselves are perfect, or that every woman we meet has the same nurturing and loving qualities that have been praised here. There are women, as we have seen, who still believe (to some extent) that men are 'better', that women are 'silly', who don't understand the importance of women's solidarity as the source of their personal strength and women's power. But probably these attitudes are becoming less common – even almost disappearing, at least on a conscious level.

The possibilities are enormous, if we can just open our eyes: if we *look* at our women friends, we will see each other in a whole new light.

Note to readers:

If you feel like sharing your answers to any of the questions in this book, or your opinions on any of the topics raised, we would be delighted to hear from you.

Please send your letters to:

Hite Research International
PO Box 5282
FDR Station
New York
NY 10022
USA

About the authors

Shere Hite graduated with a master's degree *cum laude* in history from the University of Florida then studied for her doctorate in history at Columbia University in New York. She became actively involved in the feminist movement during the 1970s, and in 1976, after five years' research, published the ground-breaking *The Hite Report on Female Sexuality*. This work was the first to document in women's own voices the reality of their sexual lives, to state explicitly that the definition of sex as 'intercourse' is socially and culturally constructed, not biologically ordained, and to create a new theory about the nature of sexuality. *The Hite Report on Female Sexuality* became an international bestseller, and later, along with *The Hite Report on Male Sexuality*, won an award for distinguished service from the American Association of Sex Educators, Counsellors and Therapists.

From 1977 to 1989 Hite travelled extensively in Europe, Asia and the United States, including those countries in which her books are banned, speaking about women's place in history and researching the final two parts of her now classic trilogy, *The Hite Report on Male Sexuality* and *The Hite Report on Women and Love*. *Women and Love*, based on the testimony of 4,500 women, is the first work to document the extent of entrenched emotional violence against women, and to document women themselves in the process of re-naming and redefining the cultural ideology of 'love'. Hite's view of women's thinking as 'a cultural revolution in progress' was considered highly controversial, and became an international *cause célèbre* in 1987–8, leading to the formation of a defense committee for her in 1988.

Shere Hite has taught at the University of Florida and New York University, and has received numerous honorary awards. She is listed in the 1978 *World Almanac* as one of the twenty-five most influential women in America. Hite is also well-known for her philanthropic work, and she is currently active in the ecology movement, writing a satirical novel including ecological themes.

She is married to the German classical pianist Friedrich Höricke and lives in New York.

Kate Colleran was born in New York in 1959 and grew up in England. She returned to the United States in 1977. Graduating from Smith College, Massachusetts, in English Literature, she has been involved in publishing and the acting world, and has worked for Shere Hite.

Kate Colleran, who is the daughter of actress Lee Remick, has travelled extensively throughout the world and is now based in New York. She married Pike Sullivan in 1989.